Dr. Stephanie

Relationship Repair for Couples

A Customer Service Approach for Minimizing Conflict and Creating Lasting Love in Your Relationships

2/8/15

Austin and Savannah,

Best of Luck to your Marriage!
Always Keep your Repair Counter
in Top-Top Shape!

Dr. Stephanie Weiland Knarr

Dr. Stephanie's Motto:
"Less Drama and More Success in Your Relationships."

Dr. Stephanie's
Relationship Repair for Couples

A Customer Service Approach for Minimizing Conflict and Creating Lasting Love in Your Relationships

Stephanie Weiland Knarr PhD, LCMFT

HEARTLAND EAST
Publishing

Fulton, MD

For information, address the publisher:
www.drstephanieonline.com
Heartland East Publishing
c/o CMI
13518 L Street
Omaha, NE 68137

Paperback ISBN: 978-0-9864443-1-9
Kindle ISBN: 978-0-9864443-2-6
Epub ISBN: 978-0-9864443-3-3

Library of Congress Control Number on file with the publisher

Printed in the United States of America.

10 9 8 7 6 5 4 3 2 1

To Brendan Knarr, my devoted husband. Thank you for having your Relationship Repair Counter open—even late at night!

Contents

———•———

Introduction

A business cannot succeed without providing prompt and skilled customer service that resolves complaints. Without customer service to fix the mistakes that humans inevitably make, trust and security are lost, and customers will eventually choose to conduct business elsewhere.

Likewise, a committed personal and romantic relationship cannot succeed without two people, both with an attitude of prompt and caring service for their significant other's complaints. Research on marriage communication by the Gottman Institute has found that one of the primary causes of America's high divorce rate is that the spouses are not being influenced by each other's complaints. Essentially, my interpretation of this is that the "customer service departments" of our marriages are failing miserably.

Well, I think it is time we change that! I'm Dr. Stephanie Weiland Knarr, and I want to introduce to you a new approach that I call *Relationship Repair for Couples*. This proven technique (or way of looking at committed relationships) is meant to inspire an attitude of service toward our personal committed relationships. We can tap into skills that we already use in our business and military cultures.

Worldwide, America has a leading business economy complete with excellent customer service. Now, Relationship Repair takes an innovative approach to help couples transfer the service-oriented attitude and skills they already have in their successful business life right into their marriage and personal relationships.

I urge you to have an effective and prompt customer service approach in your committed relationship.

Relationship Repair for Couples is a straightforward book meant to inspire an American attitude of service within couples' relationships. The strategies and steps that are taught in this book can be used to increase the success of any committed relationship—for example, in dating interactions while preparing for marriage, within committed romantic partnerships, and for those who are legally married.

In this book, I teach you how to apply business customer service skills to the future success of your romantic relationships. I promise to teach what you need to know in order to have less drama and conflict in your life as a couple.

When I refer to a committed relationship, I am talking about two people who love each other and have created a life together. They have made a commitment to each other in every way: social, physical, mental, and spiritual. Most readers will be married couples, but we know that committed relationships can exist without the legal designation of marriage. I address all of you without judgment.

Future books in this series will address Relationship Repair in other settings such as with coworkers and with your children and other family members.

This book is strictly about you and your partner. I use the terms *significant other, partner, mate, husband, wife* and *spouse* interchangeably to refer to this type of romantic commitment. I even call it your love life, but please understand, this is not a sex manual (although I guarantee if you're getting along and resolving conflicts, your bedroom may be a happier place).

I will also use *he* and *she* examples from time to time to avoid that awkward he/she thing.

In short, the Relationship Repair concepts within this book can be used for any couple who wants to have less conflict and a more successful and lasting relationship.

You will notice that this book is short because I hope that it can be helpful to many people, possibly even to those "men from Mars" who may be less inclined to read long self-help books.

The concepts of Relationship Repair are based upon solid experience and research. I have been conducting couples therapy for over a decade after completing both a master's degree and a doctorate in marriage and family therapy. I have been running my own business since 2002, and I was raised by parents who are small business owners. I am also the wife of a businessman.

My husband, Brendan Knarr, has also influenced some of the concepts within this book. He claims that this is a "well-balanced book" because it includes the husband and businessman's perspective. Brendan has been involved in business for nearly twenty years. He obtained a bachelor of science degree in business and government with a minor in psychology from Shippensburg University of Pennsylvania. Brendan is currently a successful sales manager for a large steel company.

Here is the honest to goodness truth. I can talk all day long about why I think having a Relationship Repair Counter is important to help change the divorce rate, but I have spent a lot of time developing this concept for very personal reasons. I am a passionate person, and I have been known to be the agitated customer or the agitated girlfriend when my complaints are not resolved.

Some people handle conflict more gracefully than I. Even though I think I am generally a very good wife, my husband Brendan is a salesperson and he is a talker. So there is no shortage of complaints that he makes at my Relationship Repair Counter. I am also not conflict avoidant, and I have no problem filing complaints at Brendan's Relationship Repair Counter. The point is this: I can see what happens when complaints are serviced well, and I can see what happens when they are not. When they are not, I have been known on rare occasion to end up sleeping on the couch. When complaints are addressed, there are peaceful sweet dreams.

Given my clinical experience, I know for a fact that I am not the only spouse alive who has had both good and bad experiences resolving complaints and problems.

I have also had the Relationship Repair experience in my private practice by helping married couples for nearly fifteen years, and I can give you a plethora of examples of what happens when a female files a complaint and her man dismisses her or gets defensive instead of providing proper service—or vice versa—for example:

- Sadness and withdrawal, quiet resentment
- Crying and helplessness
- Anger, verbal assaults
- Threats to end a relationship
- One person leaving the bedroom or the house
- Sometimes an escalation of conflict leading to physical violence
- Verbal fighting
- Texting wars
- Drinking or smoking
- Infidelities out of revenge

If you have experienced any of these problems after filing a relationship complaint or after hearing your mate file a complaint, then this Relationship Repair approach is for you. What this means is that you are having problems with conflict resolution with your partner. However, this is a typical and treatable problem.

To figure out if you may need some more help with resolving conflict in your relationship, answer the following questions:

- Are your disagreements resolved quickly?
- Would you say that when you finish having a disagreement with your mate, that you feel resolved and have no resentments?

- When your spouse is upset, do you start out by saying, "You are important to me, and I don't like to see you so upset"?

- When your spouse is complaining (about your behavior or about something else), do you listen without interrupting?

- Do you regularly ask your mate, "What can I do to resolve this for you?" or "What can I do to comfort you?"

- Do you ask your husband or wife if you have made them feel better or if you have fully resolved their concern?

- When your spouse is upset, do you engage in reflective listening, such as saying, "So, your concern is _____? Is that right?"

If you answered no to many of these questions, then Relationship Repair is definitely for you. You will notice that some of the questions point to whether or not you are applying customer service skills to your romantic relationship.

I would now like to share with you a little bit about how Relationship Repair developed.

Solution-focused marriage therapists, like myself, help people to creatively learn to transfer strengths and solutions used in one part of their life to another. So in my work as a couples therapist, I started to use the metaphor of business customer service (something that many of my clients are successful at doing) as a solution to help people improve their skills at resolving complaints within their committed relationships.

This metaphor of having a customer service counter for marriage started out as a simple, creative solution that I tried with one couple. The husband was a highly successful businessman who was excellent at repairing customer complaints, but he was terrible at servicing his wife's complaints.

I tried this metaphor, and it clicked. It was one of those light bulb moments. This couple liked the concept so much I tried it with other couples. My clients were extremely receptive to these metaphors, and I found myself using the metaphor of a "customer service counter" for resolving marriage complaints on a regular basis—and the concept of the Relationship Repair Counter was born.

Thinking of couples within a business framework was second nature to me because we family systems therapists are trained to think of family organizations as having similar organizational and systemic principles as other organizations—to include business, societal, and government organizations.

Another author, Dr. John Curtis, wrote *The Business of Love*. As a marriage therapist and business consultant, he also encourages couples to apply business concepts to their romantic relationships. However, Dr. Curtis is focused on assisting couples with creating a vision statement, writing objectives, outlining a budget, identifying job descriptions, and scheduling review meetings. His book and approach have a different, broader focus than mine.

Relationship Repair for Couples is basically a customer service training manual for your romantic relationship, and I trust you will find this to be a refreshing and cutting edge look at how you think about relationship problems. By the time you are finished reading *Relationship Repair,* I want you motivated to have an attitude of service in your relationship.

When your spouse files a very sour complaint, you are going to turn that lemon into lemonade and come up with increased trust, loyalty, and fun in your love life. My mission is to start a movement that will help Relationship Repair attitudes and practices to spread because I believe that with an American attitude of service applied to our marriages, people can create far more "happily ever afters." I want you and as many Americans as possible to know the joy of true Relationship Repair success.

Chapter 1

How May I Serve You Today?

You are furious with your husband. Oh, he's a sweet guy most of the time, but right now you're steaming because he left tools all over the garage. You couldn't get your car in and had to carry all the groceries yourself. You have a complaint you want addressed, and you want it fixed right now.

So imagine yourself walking in the front door and seeing a big flashing sign that says, "Relationship Repair Counter, Open Now."

You step up to the service counter and say, "Babe, you promised to not leave your tools out but you left them all over the garage, and I had to park in the driveway and then haul in all the groceries—and with ice all over the driveway. Seriously, I could use a little help here!"

In addressing your complaint, your husband responds, "Oh my goodness, I don't want you walking on the ice. Of course, I will bring in the groceries next time. (As he laughs) I am going to have to make it up to you that I left those tools out since I promised to keep them put away."

Since the service counter was open and your husband repaired your complaint, you feel confident and secure about your relationship. Your anger is much calmer, and you also feel valued and respected.

I would be thrilled if I could tell you that most people have the security of knowing their "plus one" has an A+ Relationship Repair Counter like the husband in this example for resolving complaints, but in my experience as a relationship expert, that is simply not the case. In fact, most couples who need help with communication and regular fighting are having problems with complaint resolution.

Research in Dr. John Gottman's Love Laboratory at the University of Washington found that women make more complaints in marriage than men do (I am sure that this finding is not a surprise to most of you). And although women are known to express their complaints, we do know from other research that women and men alike are seeking greater equity in their romantic relationships. How complaints are resolved and repaired is an important predictor for ongoing relationship success.

I am going to teach you how to start your very own personal customer service desk for resolving issues with your significant other. When you have a Relationship Repair Counter, your chances for success in a romantic relationship improve greatly.

There are many good reasons for you and your partner to learn Relationship Repair skills. I want you to open your own personal Relationship Repair Counter for that special someone in your life, and I want you to do it for all the right reasons, such as these:

Reason #1 The skilled servicing of business complaints leads to business profit and success. However, customer service is a learnable skill that does not come naturally to most people. People who are skilled in business customer service have had training that helps them learn how to not withdraw or attack when irate customers are screaming complaints over the phone or standing in front of them with a lawn mower part that failed.

A business that is primarily profit-oriented and does not listen to the needs of the customer (in other words, the business is not service-oriented) often does not thrive long term. Likewise, romantic relationships thrive only when couples are service-oriented. Successful couples build skills that allow them to listen and resolve their partners' complaints as well as showing interest in the overall wellness of their mate.

Reason #2 Marriage research shows that the skilled servicing of complaints is one of the primary predictors for relationship success.

Drs. John M. and Julie S. Gottman are leading experts on marital communication. Together they founded and direct the Gottman Institute in Seattle, Washington (gottman.com). Dr. John Gottman found in his reputable research on married couples that one of the major predictors for divorce is the following: Husbands are failing to "be influenced" by their wives' complaints and concerns. Also, wives are not using "slow start-up" when they communicate complaints to their husbands. "Slow start-up" is a research term that describes the behaviors of women who file complaints in a calm, less reactive manner. Although research shows that wives typically bring more complaints to the marriage relationship and that a common predictor for a failed relationship is a husband not being influenced by his wife's complaints, my observation is that both men and women benefit from improving how they service their partners' complaints. Of course, in some relationships, I have observed that a husband brings up more complaints than does his wife.

The United States has one of the highest divorce rates in the world. This fact tells me that the service counters of American marriages are failing to meet peoples' needs. In earlier generations, even if complaints were not resolved, it was not socially acceptable to get a divorce. However, times have changed and now there are many people who stay married only if they are happy and satisfied in their relationship. It has now become imperative, according to research, and per social norms for couples to have a Relationship Repair Counter for resolving complaints and problems.

Reason #3 There are many people who are successful in their business and work life who are failing in their personal romantic relationships. In many cases, people are not transferring good business skills into their partnership communication.

During my work with couples for over fifteen years, I have become more and more intrigued about this fact: Many men who are effectively able to respond to customer complaints in their business, professional, and work life struggle to do so effectively with their wife or girlfriend. Many women who are effectively able to get complaints resolved in their consumer and work life struggle to do so in their romantic life with their husband or boyfriend.

There is simply no good reason for this. In many cases, people already have the skills to resolve conflict because they do it in their business life. I see it as my mission to help people use the same skill set within their romantic relationships.

Reason #4 Through *Relationship Repair*, readers will find a helpful review of business service principles and skills for corporate employees and small business people who want to improve or freshen up their business service skills and improve their ability to juggle work and family life.

Reason #5 Even if your romantic relationship is satisfactory now, following the attitudes and steps in *Relationship Repair* is an ideal way to prevent future relationship problems and maintain a happy partnership. Learning the skills necessary to maintain a happy romantic relationship is also a smart financial decision.

Yes, sometimes people are thinking of marriage entirely from a romantic or sexual perspective, and they forget about the business end of things. Marriage is still a legal contract. Quite simply, it is a financially sound business decision to maintain a happy marriage. Why? Because divorce and the division of assets can be costly to your financial future.

I hope that I have now persuaded you that having a customer service counter for your romantic relationship is vital to its success and longevity.

**There is simply no reason for the
divorce rate to continue as it is!
Americans *know* service.
You *know* service.**

Here are some points to support the fact that Americans already have a great attitude about service.

- America thrives on a service-oriented economy.

- America's military men and women protect our liberties and serve our country well.

- Americans show honor and appreciation for the service attitudes of our police and firefighters.

- The diverse religions that make up America all encourage an attitude of service. For example, Christian scripture narrates Jesus modeling humility and service when he washed the feet of his disciples at the Last Supper.

We owe it to our partners and our children to transfer our service attitudes and skills right into our intimate relationships at home. What makes me even more excited about the concepts within *Relationship Repair* is that families can role model for children the service skills that they will need in the adult business world. Therefore, the interchangeable skills of Relationship Repair can be used to increase American success in business, community, *and* family life.

You might be thinking: What about people who have not had business training in customer service? How will the concepts offered in this book help these individuals transfer business skills into their marriage? To answer this question, consider that Relationship Repair also helps people transfer skills and communication that they see and hear literally every day as consumers. And we all know there are few Americans who are not good consumers.

I think Americans simply have a different attitude and response in our business, consumer, and work life, than we do in our romantic, marriage, and family relationships. Most people have great intentions. After all, people who get married vow to love, honor, and care for one another. A woman, for example, doesn't vow that she will love and honor her spouse except for when her husband complains about her! Instead, she vows that she will love, honor, and serve her spouse all the time, *even when he complains.*

So I am suggesting that we have our vows say, "I promise to love, honor, and *serve* you." Love and honor are often thought of as feeling words. The words *love* and *honor* are tied up with ribbons and bows and all kinds of romantic notions for most people.

Make no mistake though; the word *serve* is undoubtedly an action word. As soon as you hear the word *serve*, don't you think about "doing, helping, fixing, protecting"? Imagine if we used the word *serve* in our marriage vows? How many more marriages would be successful if we were to change our attitudes about servicing our partners' complaints?

In the upcoming chapters, I will be teaching you the attitudes and skills that you need for having an effective Relationship Repair Counter for your committed relationship.

I have found that many people who engage in marriage counseling absolutely have an attitude of service in their work, religious, and civic life. These are the kinds of people, for example, whose eyes well up with tears and thoughts of patriotic service to country when they hear "The Star-Spangled Banner." But somehow that attitude of service just doesn't translate when their mate rings the bell at the Relationship Repair Counter.

Granted, I understand that hearing the Relationship Repair bell can be difficult. You most likely feel more vulnerable at home, in your personal life. It can be hard to hear your partner complain about you. After all, you much prefer kissing, date nights, and making love. But if you have not figured this out already, your partner is going to complain about you sometimes. Sometimes your spouse will take your character flaws, whatever they might be, and try to steer you in a different direction. Or, sometimes, your mate might simply be having a grouchy day.

So, really, if you want to have a significant other in your life, then you have a choice to make. You can either choose to create an effective and prompt Relationship Repair Counter for your partner's concerns, making it more likely that your romantic relationship will last. Or you can fail at having a Relationship Repair Counter and wait until every last ounce of trust has been lost, possibly dooming your relationship to failure.

If you choose not to recognize potential problems and resolve issues when your mate rings the Relationship Repair bell, the trust in the relationship slowly deteriorates. Sooner or later, your mate may give up altogether.

When I say your mate will give up, I think there is usually one of three devastating consequences:

- Even if your partner remains committed to you, you will never know how happy your relationship could have been, how romantic and delightful your wife would have been, if only you had shown her that she was a valuable and important person to you at the service counter. In other words, your love life is quite likely to be far less satisfying for both of you.

- Your partner will walk away from your relationship possibly never trusting in relationships again. He may rather live alone than to have the frustration of ringing the bell at the Relationship Repair Counter repeatedly only to find out that it is always closed—or to receive the message that he is not valued enough to have his complaints resolved.

- Your partner may leave you in pursuit of a new, trusting relationship with a partner who has a skilled relationship service department.

Let me close this chapter by acknowledging that I understand something: Listening to complaints from your partner and resolving them will not be the enjoyable part of your romantic relationship.

Similarly, any small business owner will tell you that resolving complaints is not why they went into business. Most went into business to provide a service or product that they enjoy providing. Furthermore, most business owners went into business to make a profit.

People commit to a partner because they yearn for a mate, for companionship, for children, passion, and for greater financial security. No one ever says, "I know. I'll get involved in a relationship so I can repair complaints!"

The point is that complaint resolution is not what people are thinking about when they start a business or a romantic relationship. In fact, servicing complaints will likely be one of the most difficult, least pleasurable parts of your job as a mate. But I am recommending that you become successful at this part of your job description.

Having a Relationship Repair Counter that works properly is 100 percent necessary in order to keep the relationship you desire for all of the *other* reasons I just mentioned, such as being a helpmate, seeking companionship, feeling passion, having children, and gaining greater financial security.

Anyone who has ever had to be a customer service representative knows that it is far easier to handle complaints after being trained with the proper skills and tools. *Relationship Repair* can help you learn the skills you need and make it easier to resolve your mate's complaints. This is my mission. Now, let me teach you how to take the skills you already use in your business and consumer life and apply those to your committed relationship.

Chapter 2

————— ✦ —————

Where Is Your Customer Service Counter?

A man walks into Home Depot. He's carrying a ceiling fan in a box. The greeter at the door says, "Hello, sir. Welcome to Home Depot. May I help you find something?"

"Yes," the customer says. "I'd like to return this fan. It doesn't work. Where is the customer service counter?"

"Oh, I'm sorry, sir," says the greeter. "We don't have one."

"Well, what am I supposed to do about my problem?"

"I just don't know, sir. But we're having a special on appliances. May I direct you to that department?"

"What?" the man starts yelling.

Have you ever felt as frustrated and devalued as this customer when it comes to your relationship? Well, if you are like many couples, you have experienced situations when your significant other does not have a customer service counter for your complaints about the relationship.

I want you to think about whether or not you and your partner have a customer service counter (or what I like to a call a Relationship Repair Counter) for each other's complaints?

To answer this question, think about how you usually react when that special someone in your life files a complaint—

especially if it is about something *you* did (or didn't do). Or think about how you react when that same special someone appears upset, angry, or moody.

I have observed that, quite often, people respond poorly to these kinds of situations. In fact, some people completely ignore or dismiss their partner's complaints and moods. Certain behaviors basically tell your mate that you do not have a Relationship Repair Counter. They are

- Shutting down and not saying anything

- Rolling your eyes

- Changing the topic to something else more pleasant

- Shifting the topic to a complaint that you have about your spouse (Sure, you can bring up complaints, but I recommend you start with resolving your partner's complaint first.)

- Strongarming your partner by dominating the conversation, taking all the air time, or talking over your partner

- Telling your mate that you do not understand why he feels that way. In fact, he "should" not even have the complaint that he is making.

- Focusing on the manner in which your partner is filing the complaint. For example, that they are not being calm and constructive.

Do you often display any of these behaviors when your partner complains? If you do, then I highly recommend that you learn new ways to react. Instead, I urge you to open up your Relationship Repair Counter.

I am extremely passionate about helping you see relationship complaints from your partner in a completely new light. Please remember that avoiding or dismissing the complaints of your significant other is similar to a business not having a customer service department to assist our customer with the broken fan. Can you even imagine that scenario?

Let's think about this for a minute. Imagine yourself being that consumer with a problem, and you walk into the place of business only to find out there is no customer service department. You can't believe it! There is no representative at this business who takes complaints; or there is, but she's never there. Each time you try to get your complaint resolved, you get more frustrated and angry. Also, how frustrated you are depends upon how much you need the product or service at that time.

When you add the fact that people feel emotionally, physically, and sometimes sexually vulnerable in their romantic relationships, it is completely understandable why people get angry and have fights when they think that the person they love does not value the partnership enough to have a Relationship Repair Counter.

I urge you to put yourself in the shoes of your mate. If he keeps walking to the Relationship Repair Counter only to find there is no one behind it, he is likely to become more frustrated with each attempt. Similarly, if you keep calling 1-800-NO REPAIR-COUNTER to register your complaint and no one answers, your resentment and anger is likely to build up.

Everyone in a relationship has also experienced the shoe being on the other foot, meaning that your mate is filing a complaint about you. Sometimes, the partner brings up the complaint when it is not an ideal time—if you know what I mean.

Have you ever gotten a complaint from your significant other while you are at work? This has happened to me, and it definitely throws things into a tailspin because it is difficult for my Relationship Repair Counter to be open for my husband and my clients at the same time.

It is really a bummer when I hear the phone buzz and I check between appointments, and I see that it is my husband registering a complaint via text. I assume the message will be something sweet or considerate, or it might be planning the schedule for the evening. No matter how much I believe that people absolutely must have a Relationship Repair Counter, it still catches me off guard when my husband files a complaint about me nearly every gosh darn time.

My point is that we humans do not like it when people point out our flaws. We can point out our own flaws at the right time and we readily file necessary complaints with our partner, but we don't really like it so much when someone else confronts us, do we?

In fact, in some cases our autonomic nervous system reacts and we get downright in a panic about it. We get scared of being abandoned, hurt, or embarrassed—and if you are not conscious of those feelings, that is my job. Whether you are conscious of it or not, there is a part of you that feels afraid and vulnerable when someone files a complaint about you. Will they give you a chance to fix it? Will they punish you for it? Will they still like you? These are likely some of the underlying subconscious thoughts and feelings you have the minute your partner tells you she does not like how your issues are causing problems in her life.

Let me give you a relationship complaint example from my personal life that has also come up in my private practice. I can tell you that I have had more than one client complain that their significant other is occasionally absent minded. As they are going over the laundry list of transgressions their spouse has had, I am thinking for a moment about my own faults. You see, I am known to be processing a lot of different *feelings* in my head, so sometimes I am not paying attention to what is going on around me as much as I ought to. I do something absent minded that affects my husband.

For example, a few years ago not long after moving into our new house, I left the garage door open one day when I left to run an errand. My husband, Brendan, came home to an open garage door. A burglar or a murderer could have just walked right in! My husband is very protective and concerned about safety, even more than I. On occasion if I have a lot on my mind, I can do something like this and it understandably freaks him out. It upsets me too that I could leave the garage door open accidentally, but since I am the one who has control over my own actions, it is less upsetting for me than it is for him.

I remember getting the sick feeling in my stomach when he told me how upset he was. He went into "parent" mode and starting telling me all the reasons why this was not cool. I have seen people respond in the right way and the wrong way to these kinds of situations.

Right way: "Of course you know I would never leave the garage door open on purpose, but even so I am really sorry. I want you to trust me, so I will really try to never make that mistake again. Is there anything else I can do to make this right with you?" This normally defuses the situation and the focus becomes on resolution.

Wrong way: Rolling eyes. "Everybody makes mistakes. It was an accident and you make mistakes too. Remember the day you left the back door unlocked?"

This response usually escalates the situation and the couple begins fighting back and forth about various mistakes each has made and who is more absent minded in the relationship. Sometimes this kind of fight or a series of similar fights can even ruin a whole evening or a whole weekend or a whole relationship, which is actually pretty sad.

You might be thinking, "What kind of complaint is the doctor talking about?" Complaints can encompass so many different kinds of problems and occurrences that it is impossible for me to list them all. However, let me give you a list here just so I can make sure we are on the same page.

Common relationship complaints among couples that I have seen in my private practice include these areas:

- Being late to an agreed upon meeting without calling or texting to explain

- Quitting or losing too many jobs

- Not remembering to do something special for a birthday or anniversary

- Making too many negative, critical comments and not enough positive or appreciative comments

- Leaving a mess in the bathroom sink
- Yelling at the kids too much
- Spending more time with friends than with the partner
- Making large purchases without consulting the other person
- Not answering the phone
- Not planning date nights or quality time together
- Spending too much time online on Facebook
- Not having sex with enough frequency or passion
- Not having a Relationship Repair Counter

Something that might cause a complaint for one person might not be a complaint for someone else. The concerns and complaints that I hear in the couples therapy room are so many and varied that I could write a relationship complaint dictionary. What is important is that the complaint resolutions are reasonable and that partners value each other enough to honor reasonable suggested resolutions.

Throughout this book, I will introduce you to couples I have encountered in my practice. Of course, names and situations are altered to protect my clients' privacy. Meet Vinay and Serena.

Case Example: Vinay and Serena

Vinay and Serena described themselves as a loving and committed married couple. They had successful careers and three children still living at home. However, they explained they were seeking help for a recent conflict that had escalated. They went on to tell me they have had a pattern of fights that escalates every couple of months. Both agreed that the fights were so difficult and lengthy that they felt it took time to recover. They wanted to stop this pattern so it wouldn't continue to disrupt their family life. The couple also wanted to improve their attempts to not fight in front of the children.

Serena's complaint: Vinay failed to answer the phone during an urgent incident when she really needed him. Vinay looked at me with the telepathic message that his wife was unreasonable, and he went on to defend himself with the wrong response: "I sometimes do answer the phones. I forgot to take it off quiet mode, so I did not know the phone was ringing. And it is unrealistic for her to expect that I will always be able to answer."

In a nutshell, Vinay's response to Serena's complaint was that her complaint was not valid according to him, and that was that. I then observed Serena starting to sob as she complained that whenever she brings up complaints, she typically does not get a resolution.

After some work and discussion, I assisted Vinay to open his Relationship Repair Counter, and he really listened. He ultimately asked Serena, "What can I do to resolve your complaint?"

Ultimately, Serena wanted Vinay to show understanding and empathy for why she was so devastated on this particular occasion that he did not pick up the phone. Most importantly, she wanted Vinay to agree to be more attentive to answering the phone when she calls.

As Vinay agreed to these resolutions he was then able to negotiate with Serena a bit as well. Serena was able to acknowledge that it is not always reasonable for her husband to be there at all times, but she appreciated his agreement to try to improve his attentiveness.

Now, let's assume that, like Vinay, even though you want to make your wife happy and try to fix the problems she has brought to you, somehow the conversations keep resulting in a fight. When this occurs, it could be similar to your speaking with a business customer service representative who has not had the proper training. Since they do not use the right customer service skills, they actually say things that make you become even more frustrated or upset. This likely conjures up all kinds of images in your mind. Perhaps you can think of times when you have been the agitated customer, or perhaps you are Mr. Easy Going and you are often the one laughing at the agitated customers' antics while waiting in line.

In any case, the point is that the person you are in love with might not be Mr. Easy Going and he might not respond well to not having the proper skills at the Relationship Repair Counter. No worries! I will be teaching you new ways to react to the complaints and feelings of your partner throughout the rest of this book.

Relationship Repair is meant to teach you the right attitudes and skills to resolve complaints in your relationship. In the next chapter, I will be teaching you service attitudes that will help you at the Relationship Repair Counter. In a later chapter, I will teach you the specific steps that will help you to effectively register and repair those relationship complaints.

Chapter 3

———◆———

"Service after the sale"? Are You Kidding Me?

After ten rings, the phone is answered with a canned message, "The menu has changed, so please listen carefully. For billing, press 1. For transfer of service, press 2. For repair, press 3." You press 3.

"Repair."

"Yes," you ask, "is this department that handles cell phone upgrades? I wasn't offered that choice on the menu."

"Um, well, no, this is repair. But let me transfer you."

"Where are you ..." (On-hold music for three minutes.)

"Billing."

"I'm trying to upgrade my cell phone. Who handles that?"

"We're billing, ma'am. Let me get you to the right person."

"Wait, wait, wait ..."

Sound familiar? Attitude is everything; however, you will notice in this example no one really listened to the customer or made sure the customer's needs were going to be met. No one was helpful to the caller, and no one demonstrated a helpful attitude either.

This chapter is basically a cognitive therapy exercise. I want you to think about what you were thinking and what you felt when your significant other made a recent complaint. Stop and think of at least three examples.

If you are like most people, you are going to notice that you have some negative thoughts and attitudes that come up when you think about your spouse filing a complaint about you. So I want to teach you some helpful attitudes to counteract current unhelpful thoughts. This chapter offers six Relationship Repair attitude adjustments.

Over the years observing people's reactions in marriage and couples therapy, I have noted that men and women have various unhelpful thoughts and attitudes about relationship complaints. One of the most powerful negative perceptions for relationship success is to think this: "We have a bad relationship if my partner is bringing up complaints about me." This is simply not true.

No matter how happy your relationship is or how good it is, relationship complaints that require repair are inevitable.

> **Relationship Repair Attitude #1: Even though you are a terrific mate, it is normal for your partner to complain.**

Let me put the truth right out there. Even if you are an excellent partner in many ways, you are not perfect. Most people will absolutely admit they are not perfect, and yet people get so mad when their significant other points out their imperfections.

If you sometimes think that relationship complaints mean your relationship is doomed and "on the rocks," then I have news for you. You absolutely must change your thinking because it is actually the job of your significant other to help you grow as a person and also to ask you to make adjustments for her own needs so she does not end up building resentment. In particular, the adjustments you are asked to make are sometimes due to a personality weakness you have.

If you are a woman, think of it this way. You frequent a small boutique that has exclusive products. The owner is very adept at creating a wonderful atmosphere and purchasing unique items for her customers. The staff is pleasant and the boutique is in a convenient location. However, the owner has a weakness. She is so focused on the creative part of her business that she has failed to create an efficient system for handling returns and refunds.

So, even though you like the boutique location, the atmosphere, and the products, you have made complaints about how her employees respond to returns. It may take many complaints and adjustments from numerous customers before the boutique owner gets her system improved.

Your romantic relationship is the same way. Your partner is likely to ask you to improve parts of yourself that need more work. This does not mean that you are not being a great wife, or that you don't have many positive qualities. It just means you have room for improvement. As you go through the life cycle, you will inevitably need to make new adjustments to meet different life situations.

And, for men, since I know you could not resist reading the previous information for women, you may already have gotten the point. If not, try thinking of it this way. Let's say you are an avid car collector and you regularly take your vehicles to be serviced, maintained, and repaired at a local mechanic's shop. The mechanic is an honest guy, and he has a reputation for telling the truth about what is wrong with your vehicles and how much it will reasonably cost to repair them.

But the owner has a weakness. He is sociable and good-natured. He has extended conversations with every customer who walks through the door. As a result, his shop is inefficient and it takes half the day to get your automobile serviced. Even though you like his store location, trustworthiness, and friendliness, you complain to the owner about how long you have to wait for the service. It may take many complaints and adjustments before he learns that his customers prefer efficiency over his friendliness.

On the other hand, your mechanic's competitor across town may not be as personable and is more expensive, but he gets the job done more efficiently, which frees up time in your schedule. This is appealing to you. Now, I am not telling you to run out and switch mechanics or spouses, but rather to register your complaints and also work on your own weaknesses.

You are not human if you don't have your character flaws. In fact, there is a good chance that you will be a better, more well-rounded person if you hear your partner's concerns and make adjustments to improve your personal weaknesses.

Case Example: Juanita and Martin

Juanita complains that she and Martin had a huge fight over money. She complained that Martin forgot to pay the joint credit card bill on time for the past two months, and the mistake put a ding in her credit scores. Juanita is very responsible with money and protecting her credit so she was furious at her husband.

He looks extremely annoyed and responds by saying, "Good grief. You are acting all crazy over one time that I forgot to do something? Normally I remember to pay the bills just fine."

Let's look at what is wrong with this response. Imagine if a restaurant owner were to tell a customer, "Good grief, the last eight times you came to our restaurant we gave you perfect service and a great meal. Now the one time that we screwed up your order, you are going to complain? Are you crazy?"

Fortunately, this is not how most business owners and managers handle complaints. If so, they would be dismissing the customer's concerns and would probably lose business quickly. Rather, successful business owners generally strive for a customer to be satisfied all the time. They know that customer satisfaction is not always going to exist, but it is their goal. If their company makes a mistake, normally the business person will listen, apologize, and make it up to their customer via a free product or some other incentive to maintain and rebuild the relationship.

In your romantic relationship with a significant other, the fact of the matter is that even if you are getting things right 95 percent of the time, your partner may still have a complaint when you make a mistake. This is normal. Sometimes, you may not hear enough appreciation for the 95 percent of the time you are doing things correctly. In this case, you can ask your partner for more appreciation by filing a complaint at their Relationship Repair Counter. However, it is still imperative that you service your partner's complaints.

> **Relationship Repair Attitude #2: If your partner complains, consider it a good thing. It means she is still doing business with you. Be ready to service relationship complaints.**

Okay, I realize that this is really turning lemons into lemonade. After all, it's pretty sour hearing your husband tell you he thinks that you are becoming a Facebook addict. Or, men, hearing your wife tell you that you are turning into a caveman.

I've noticed most people do not like to hear their spouse complain about them, *especially when the complaining partner is right.* In this scenario, the unhelpful reasoning can be to think that your mate does not love you anymore and does not want to be close to you. I have heard people describe that they sometimes feel this way upon hearing they have disappointed their partner. However, this is not true at all. In fact, the opposite is true.

This is the good news. If your significant other is still ringing the Relationship Repair bell, it means you are in business. You are in a relationship with your mate. Your mate still has a trusting relationship with you, and she is reaching out to you so that you can be closer by repairing a problem.

When your partner rings your service bell, it means she still believes in you, likes you, and thinks you are going to help resolve her concerns. And if you love your sweetie, then this is a good problem to have. It is a much worse problem if your partner has completely stopped doing business with you via no longer registering complaints, and has emotionally checked out of the relationship.

Even though it is not really that pleasant to repair a relationship complaint, it is important to use this lemon as lemonade, as an opportunity for you to get closer to your mate and to build loyalty with each other.

Case Example: Meet Jimmy and Erin

Jimmy and Erin learned about loyalty after several years of marriage conflict. Erin came to therapy saying that she was tired of telling Jimmy problems, and then he turned the problem into something else. She said most problems she had complained about had not been resolved for six years.

I observed that Jimmy would get hurt and then start complaining that Erin was attacking him. He said he felt that she did not like him and that she was just trying to pick a fight with him.

After several conversations, Jimmy was finally able to see that Erin was actually trying to be closer by trying to fix what she saw as a problem. He learned to be patient and to ask her how he could help make things right with her. Once they figured that out, Erin was thrilled with Jimmy. He was able to see how his changed attitude about marriage complaints helped the couple to grow even closer.

Servicing a customer's complaint takes patience and the ability to really focus attention on the customer and to find out what the ideal resolution is. Customer service research shows that a business is not seen in a positive light by a customer right after a mistake. However, it is important to know that as soon as the company repairs the mistake effectively, the customer actually has more loyalty to the business than before the mistake was made.

When your spouse makes a complaint, you can build loyalty by repairing the problem right away. This means it is very important to put down your cell phone, shut off the television, and put away anything else that might have you preoccupied. Or, if you are in the middle of something else that just cannot wait, try to see if your spouse is willing to schedule a future time to discuss the matter when your Relationship Repair Counter is open and you are not preoccupied. You can use a mistake and a complaint as an opportunity to build closeness, trust, and loyalty with your partner. It is all in how you think about it.

Relationship Repair Attitude #3: Being in a committed relationship does not mean that you can stop doing good business.

Imagine that saleswoman Jeanie courts a new account. During the courtship, she promises that her company has a great product and that she will provide good service. Eventually, her courting pays off, and she signs a contract with her new customer. Jeanie then still has to follow through on the promises she made to her customer during the courtship. Would it make sense for her to not keep her promise of providing a great product and service? Well, of course not. Eventually, that might lead to the loss of the customer relationship and potentially the entire account.

Similarly, after you are in a committed relationship, you have to keep servicing your partner. Whatever you promised your partner during your courtship needs to be delivered for years to come. If you do not keep your promises, eventually that could lead to the loss of your partnership. However, sometimes how you service your partner may change over time and new promises may need to be made. For example, Xavier told me his long-term girlfriend Laticia complained that he was spending too much money, yet she never complained while they were dating.

I have news for you: if you think that complaints later in a relationship are going to be the same as earlier in the relationship, you would be mistaken. This is not likely! Here's why. When you were courting, you were undoubtedly more attentive. The relationship was at a different level, and your mate was likely not feeling as vulnerable or as dependent. After the commitment is made, the vulnerability increases, the dependence goes up, and the attentiveness goes down. That is a recipe for more complaints. New agreements and promises will need to be negotiated as the relationship progresses in time.

One good business practice in sales is to conduct regular "checking in" with customers. Proactively following up in a customer-based relationship makes a customer feel valued. However, quite the opposite happens in couples. People often make the mistake of becoming complacent in their romantic relationships instead of staying proactive. They start thinking they've "tied the knot"—the deal is already sealed. In this case, a husband and wife mistakenly assume that the spouse will stay with them because of the marital promise, and they both lose focus on what they promised to do.

Sadly, this scenario is sometimes a mistaken assumption. I cannot tell you the number of clients whom I have seen in individual therapy right after their husband or wife has walked out the door and filed for divorce. Some of my clients state something to the effect, "I never thought my spouse would leave me."

When I take time to break down the situation, I find that my client assumed her partner (or his partner) would honor the marriage commitment "till death do us part." But when I explore further, I often find out that my client who has just been "left" was not honoring her marriage contract to love, honor, and serve. She was almost always able to tell me numerous problems in the marriage that went unresolved. In other words, she was not continuing to be attentive and proactive, and she simply was *not doing good business*. Because she was not thinking of her marriage as a contractual relationship that needed servicing, her partner ended up filing for divorce.

If you want to remain in a marriage or otherwise committed romantic relationship, then I strongly urge you to stay focused on doing "good business" and satisfying your partner. This is a reminder of what I taught you earlier in Relationship Repair —to love, honor, and care for means to serve. In order to keep your romantic relationship happy, you are required to have humility and to open up your customer service counter for your mate. In essence, you continue to court your partner and provide good business service so that the relationship stays positive, trusting, and satisfying.

> **Relationship Repair Attitude #4: If you do not properly respond to relationship complaints, your partner may not want to shop at your store as often.**

Think about it. You shop at your favorite grocery store regularly. You develop a relationship with the store manager. You stop by weekly to see what specials they have. Things are wonderful until one day you have a problem with one of the products you purchased. You approach the manager and state your complaint, hoping the problem will be fixed. The manager tells you that you are making too big a deal of things and goes back to his little manager's office and drinks his coffee.

The next time you have some grocery shopping to do, you are hesitant to conduct business at your favorite store. However, you like the products, the location, and the people so much (except for one bad experience) that you decide to give the store another try. You say to yourself, *Maybe the manager was just having a bad day.*

You again have many good experiences until there is another problem. You once again go to the manager and state your complaint. Again, he tells you "tough luck," makes you look like a pouting child, and walks back to his little manager's office to sip his coffee.

At this point, you are so annoyed that you only go back to that store if you really need a quick gallon of milk or eggs or only for specific products you can't find elsewhere such as your favorite imported wine. In fact, you can get most of the items you need from the grocery store a mile away, so you do.

This metaphor absolutely applies to your romantic relationship. If you are like the manager and dismiss your partner's complaints, he will not want to shop at your store as often. Okay, men, pay attention here. When the lights are low and the kids are in bed, you might just want your wife to shop at your store, if you know what I mean. Women, the same is true for you. When it is Sunday afternoon and you want your husband to take you and the kids on an outing to the shopping mall (he's not really into the mall scene), you may want him to help take the kids to the food court and hold the shopping bags while you are trying on clothes, if you catch my drift.

I can tell you without a shadow of a doubt that couples are typically having a much better sex life and going to more shopping malls together during the early stages of their marriage. Whatever your mate did for you at the beginning of the relationship, he is more inclined to continue those same behaviors if you properly service his complaints. When you service complaints at the Relationship Repair Counter, you create a scenario where your mate wants to keep shopping at your store.

Quite simply, this is about likeability. Partners simply do not like mates who dismiss and ignore their concerns! It is not uncommon for couples to complain in my office that when they bring up a problem, their significant other avoids them and goes into another room, leaves the house, or otherwise refuses to discuss or resolve the problem.

In marriage research by the Gottman Institute, this is referred to as stonewalling. Stonewalling is fleeing from relationship problems, and it creates a situation in which you and your mate will likely end up growing apart. If you cannot stay intimate enough to work out a problem, then the other ways you are intimate are likely to fade away also.

Meet Fabien and Carrie

Fabien and Carrie came to couples therapy each with their own list of complaints. Fabien's complaint was that Carrie was not affectionate toward him and that they had sex very infrequently. He described that he felt helpless and rejected. When I got further into the problem, I assessed for sexual dysfunction; however, this was not the problem. The couple described a great sex life earlier in the relationship.

Carrie said sex was the furthest thing from her mind because her husband was grouchy and did not listen to her. She felt he did not value her. Fabien was particularly angry that even after he took Carrie out on date nights she often rejected him. He acknowledged he could accept the rejection sometimes, but most of the time the rejection was creating a real problem for him.

After a couple of discussions we were able to pinpoint that Carrie did not have any sexual desire for her husband when he ignored her complaints at the Relationship Repair Counter, and most notably the most important complaint in her mind was that her husband was grouchy.

This couple did an amazing job learning to resolve marriage complaints, and Fabien did some of his own sessions to discuss his grouchy and critical attitude, which came from a controlling parental relationship during his growing up years.

In the end, when I checked on the couple a few months later, they had resumed a more regular sex life. Fabien was not grouchy, Carrie was hot, and both had their Relationship Repair Counters open and functioning properly.

Relationship Repair Attitude #5: If you want to figure out what your partner thinks is a fair relationship contract, listen carefully when he complains.

Simply put, marriage requires ongoing contractual negotiations. Exactly what your spouse is looking for to have a fair marriage contract will come to light in his complaints.

For example, imagine you are a gal who watched Monday night football during dating, engagement, and early marriage. But now you have a toddler in the house. Once the baby came, no more Monday night football for you! Your husband starts to complain one night that you won't snuggle up on the couch to watch NFL with him. Meanwhile, you have just finished cleaning up after dinner and are settling down your toddler for bed. You are thinking to yourself, *Good lord, how can I watch Monday night football when I am putting Charlie to sleep? He is lucky that I take care of the house and family so he can watch football.*

However, instead of saying this, you stop yourself from reacting. You open up your Relationship Service Counter and say, "Well, I want you to have fun on Monday nights since you work hard all week! Would you feel better if we spent time snuggling on the coach watching football after I get our little guy into bed or is there another way I can take care of your complaint?"

You find out rather quickly that your husband understands that you can't watch Monday night football and put the baby to bed at the same time. The resolution he suggests is that he hire a babysitter twice during the season so you can snuggle on the couch one night with popcorn, and the other night go out to watch the game at a local pub. It's a deal!

Whatever it is that your mate feels is important to the marriage contract will usually come out as a complaint. So listening to your spouse's complaints and acting on them is extremely important to having a satisfactory marriage.

> **Relationship Repair Attitude #6: Prompt and reliable Relationship Repair breeds security and trust and communicates value. Poor relationship service breeds feelings of insecurity, mistrust, and devalues your partner.**

I want you to think about yourself as a consumer with a complaint. When you make your complaint by calling up the business customer service phone number, you are either met with prompt and skilled service, or you are met with slow, unskilled service.

"Hi, this is Nicki at ABC Cable. How may I help you today?"

Wow, a real human answers the phone. Nicki sounds energetic and polite. As a result, you like ABC Cable and you feel important. You have the sense that ABC is honest. In contrast, when you call XYZ Cable, you get the automated customer support line.

"Press 1 for billing. Press 2 for service. Press 3 to hear the menu options again."

They wear you out punching in numbers and wading through various menus before you even get to state your complaint. Then, you either give up or become so frustrated because of the process that when you finally get the chance to speak with someone you come across as abrasive.

When it is finally your chance to speak, you are told that you will need to speak with a manager. Now you have to spend more time on hold. You lose trust that XYZ will ever service your complaint. You may even wonder if XYZ is cheating you with their prices because of the lack of service. You feel unimportant and uncertain about your future business dealings with XYZ.

When you are getting prompt and skilled service, you likely feel important, confident, and secure about your business relationship. When the service is slow and you are not responded to with proper assistance, you feel unimportant to that business. A loss of trust and a sense of insecurity encroach upon the business relationship.

A similar dynamic is true within romantic relationships. The better you are at providing prompt, reliable, and helpful service, the more your significant other will feel important, valued, secure, and trusting. In most cases, this will also mean a happier partner, less conflict, and more pleasant memories together. Isn't that what most of us strive for in our relationships?

On the other hand, if you are not consistent and do not provide skilled servicing of complaints, your partner is likely to start feeling unimportant and insecure and will sometimes even mistrust you. As a couples therapist, I have seen many people feeling so devalued at the Relationship Repair Counter that they also begin to wonder if their significant other is having an affair.

For example, Emily was convinced that her husband, Chad, was cheating on her. When I asked her why she thought he was cheating, she said she had never caught him speaking with other women, and she generally felt he was honest with her and she knew of his whereabouts. Clearly, in this case there was no real evidence of an infidelity; however, when engaging in couples therapy it was obvious that Chad was failing to respond to any of her complaints effectively.

We were able to identify that because Emily felt she was being devalued and dismissed at the Relationship Repair Counter, she then became suspicious about being cheated in other aspects of her relationship as well. In this case, when we worked at helping Chad to respond and resolve her complaints regarding numerous other problems in the relationship, Emily then stopped feeling so worried about infidelity.

I am hopeful that you have the intention to provide consistent service to your mate's concerns and complaints. However, ask your mate: "Do I resolve your complaints in our marriage?" If your partner says no, then read and digest the upcoming chapters. Your heart may be in the right place. You just need to learn proper Relationship Repair skills and then get some practice using them.

Chapter 4

———◆———

I'd Like to Make a Complaint

Think of yourself as a valuable partner in your committed relationship. This means that many of your concerns need to be resolved at the Relationship Repair Counter in order for you to have a happy and secure romantic relationship.

I have noticed as a couples therapist that sometimes people have positive interactions in their work life, yet when it comes to their personal relationships, they are not treated with equal value and respect. In other words, some people do not have a significant other who resolves their concerns.

My recommendation is that you follow strategies and steps at the Relationship Repair Counter similar to how you might act as a consumer at a customer service counter. I have noticed that some people, who are skilled as a consumer, do not remember to use the same strategies when they are upset with their significant other. That is, the same woman who confidently asks for a resolution to her complaint at the customer service counter in a business establishment, such as a clothing store, is an emotional wreck when seeking resolution from her romantic partner.

I would like you to think about yourself when you are upset with your partner. How do you register your complaints? Are you calm? Do you have an ideal resolution in mind before you register a complaint? I realize that most of you do not relish the task of going to the Relationship Repair Counter (nor do I). However, hopefully, you will agree with me that you are more likely to get what you want if you follow certain steps.

To help you with improving your ability to register complaints in a positive manner, imagine yourself as a consumer at the customer service counter when you are having a good day. You are calm and reasonable. You confidently ask for a resolution that you think is fair. Now, think of one of those not-so-good days—you know, the kind when you have gone to the customer service counter after you've been stuck in traffic with your kids fighting with each other in the back seat.

On those days, you are frustrated and irritated, as opposed to calm and reasonable. Now I'd like you to think about which frame of mind is most likely to lead to a positive resolution of your consumer complaint.

Naturally, when you are reasonable and follow certain thoughtful strategies, you are more likely to get your complaints resolved quickly and effectively. In fact, research from Dr. John Gottman's Love Laboratory has found that a strong predictor for marriage success is wives' using what Gottman has termed "softened start-up." Softened start-up is the ability to gently start talking about a complaint or problem with one's partner while avoiding criticism. This technique increases the likelihood that a woman's complaint will be resolved by her male counterpart. I have created several strategies for filing a complaint, which I believe can help women have slow start-up with their mates.

Now, let's walk through what these steps are and apply them to your marriage relationship.

Relationship Complaint Step #1: Think about what would resolve your complaint before you make it. Spend some time considering the following: what end result would satisfy you? Consumers are accustomed to thinking about what they want before they go to the customer service counter.

For example, consumers want a new product to replace the defective one. Or they want a refund because a product or service is not the quality they desired. In some cases, they want an apology. In other cases, they may want to know how the company will change their policies. Depending upon the circumstances, some consumers want a gift card, discount, or free product to "make up" for some kind of inconvenience that the company caused them. Some restaurants comp free desserts when they make mistakes such as overcooking a steak or forgetting the appetizer. These bonus treats are even tastier when they are free as part of the repair for making a mistake with a customer. As a consumer, you are accustomed to asking for and receiving some of the resolutions I just mentioned.

I'd like you to start applying these same principles to your committed relationship. However, in the personal arena of marriage it can be difficult if you are not accustomed to thinking in this way. I've noticed that in the complicated world of relationships, couples are less accustomed to considering what they would like as an end result. In fact, as a couples therapist I am astounded at how often I get a blank stare when I ask a woman, "What would your ideal resolution be?" She has no idea, but she has spent a considerable amount of time ruminating about her complaint.

Identify your ideal resolution in advance of registering your complaint at the Relationship Repair Counter.

In many cases, some partners have had previous romantic or family relationships (such as a parent/child or a sibling relationship) where their complaints were ignored, minimized, or met with anger or guilt trips. For these people, because of past history, they feel helpless to have their personal concerns resolved.

In essence, a person with a history of not getting their complaints addressed at the Relationship Repair Counter may anticipate never getting their complaints addressed properly in their personal life. So, ultimately, they do not even think about the resolution they are looking for from their mate. Instead, because they anticipate not being valued at the Relationship Service Counter, they build resentment and anger, and they feel very emotional and helpless. The anger and emotion spills out in the form of a complaint, and the person is actually very far away from identifying a resolution.

Meet Mary and Joe

Mary's parents did not allow her to express herself while she was growing up. If she asked for something, she was sometimes told that she was selfish. She was taught to follow parental rules, complete her chores, and go to school. If she complained about anything, she received disapproval ("You are not old enough to know what you are talking about, plus you are a spoiled brat just complaining all the time."), a guilt trip ("We are always doing things for you, but you are never satisfied."), or in some cases a punishment ("Mary, you are no longer going to be allowed to go roller skating on Friday since you are going to keep complaining.").

Fast forward. Now Mary is married to Joe, and they have three young children. She is completely overwhelmed with the busy family life of young parents, but when she and Joe have a problem, she does not complain because she learned not to set herself up for disapproval, a guilt trip, or punishment.

Therefore, her resentment grows until she is crying and upset—then her numerous complaints about Joe come spilling out. Mary has not given thought to what would resolve her complaints because she was taught as a child that she is not supposed to complain or request that someone listen to her concerns.

When Mary begins crying and bringing up her many complaints, Joe looks at her as if she is a dramazilla. He quickly becomes frustrated because he feels that Mary is having an emotional meltdown "for no reason," and he does not know how to repair her emotional complaints. Joe is anxious after a long day at work and has no idea what Mary wants him to do in order to fix the problems they are having. Joe just wants Mary to stop crying.

If Mary were to ask Joe for what she needs, her wish would be his command. He wants his wife to be happy, but he does not know how to help make her happy when she starts crying. One of the primary problems here is that Mary herself does not even know exactly what she wants to help her feel content, resolved, and peaceful. She has not identified in advance what she would ideally like for a resolution because she has been conditioned in her past relationships to not complain or ask for resolutions.

I have seen this problem frequently since becoming a relationship therapist. Quite often, a wife or husband has a complaint but a sense of helplessness sets in before they think of a resolution. Because of terrible past experiences at the Relationship Repair Counter, a wife assumes that her husband is not going to resolve her concern. So she comes to the counter already upset, emotional, and angry *without an identifiable resolution*.

If you think that you are a person who does not identify the resolution you want before you make a complaint, then it is really important that you concentrate on using this first Relationship Complaint Step. Even if you have not had good experiences getting past concerns resolved at the Relationship Repair Counter, keep in mind that your current partner may be willing to give you exactly what you are asking for in order to resolve your complaint—if only you can spell out what you need.

Give it a try by completing the following exercise: Think of a current or recent problem that you have had in your relationship that was not resolved. What outcome would make you feel better? That is, what would solve the problem for you? What is it that you would like from your partner?

Here are some common examples of resolutions in relationships for you to think about:

- Would you like an apology?

- Can you think of a new agreement you can ask your partner for that would prevent the same problem from happening in the future?

- Is there something you could ask your partner for that would help "make it up to you"?

- Would you simply like your partner to listen and verbalize that she understands your feelings about something?

- Would you like your partner to promise to discontinue a certain behavior? Or conduct a certain behavior more regularly?

Now, plan out what you will say to your partner. Practice asking for the resolution you are looking for. Give it a try, and it might actually make you feel more confident in expressing your concerns. As you are practicing this exercise, remember the following:

- You are important and valuable, and your concerns in your relationships ought to be resolved in some way.

- Your current partner might just be the kind of person who is generous and who repairs complaints. Just because you had poor relationship service in the past does not mean you will always receive poor relationship service in the future. In fact, I recommend that you invest in relationships with people who are good at repairing relationship complaints.

- If you are in a relationship with someone who does not resolve your complaints, try following the Relationship Repair complaint steps. Doing so may improve your success at getting complaints resolved. If not, you might consider requesting that your partner read this book, especially chapters 5 and 6.

Relationship Complaint Step #2: Start by saying something positive about your romantic relationship and your mate. A customer who starts out by calmly stating, "I really like doing business here because I love your products; however, I am having a problem," is more likely to get her complaint resolved.

Likewise, it is a great idea to start out by telling your significant other, for example, that you appreciate that he is a great provider before complaining that you don't like how he leaves his empty soda bottles in your vehicle. By starting out with a positive, you are increasing the chances of getting the solution you are looking for.

People like repairing problems for someone who respects and appreciates them.

The fact of the matter is that most people like repairing problems for someone who appreciates them. If you skip this second step, then you are not setting the right stage for having your complaint repaired and resolved. By expressing what you appreciate about the relationship, you are reminding your partner that you like him, respect him, and appreciate your relationship with him. This approach increases the likelihood that he will listen and resolve your complaint. By completing complaint step #2 before you actually state your complaint, you are also promoting yourself as a reasonable, respectful, and appreciative person.

Relationship Complaint Step #3: Tell your partner that you are giving him or her the benefit of the doubt. For example, you can communicate that you know she did not intentionally create this problem. *Notice here that you are now on step 3 and you have not yet stated your complaint.*

You are continuing to set the stage for appearing reasonable and calm. This is absolutely necessary for getting your complaint resolved. If you forget this step, there is a good chance that your partner is going to start explaining that she did not intend to make a mistake, frustrate you, or create a problem. Then the conversation becomes focused on intention rather than on resolution.

In a business context, a consumer might say something to the representative like, "I know you didn't create this problem," or "I know that your company did not realize that this product was defective when you sold it to me, but ..." Or another example is to say, "I am really angry right now, and I don't want to take this out on you. But you need to be aware that your company is failing at providing quality service, and I need to register my complaint."

In your romantic relationships, you will increase the likelihood of your complaint being resolved if you start out by giving your partner the benefit of the doubt. You can do this by mentioning, "I understand that you were not intentionally creating a problem." It is important that you quickly remove this potential roadblock so that you can get straight to discussing the resolution you want.

Here are some examples of things you can say to give your partner the benefit of the doubt:

- "Baby I know you don't like to upset me and you probably did not mean to hurt my feelings, but the fact is that you did."

- "You are a very good husband to me, so I know that you did not mean to create a problem, but I have a concern I'd like to address with you."

- "I know you love me and would do anything for me. So I'm trusting that you will be able to help me with this problem I'm having."

- "You are an amazing mother and you do so much for our whole family so I know you did not intend to cause a problem between us, but I want to know if I can bring a concern to the Relationship Service Counter."

Relationship Complaint Step #4: *Briefly* state only one complaint in two to three sentences. Laundry lists get dirty and convolute the real message you want to communicate.

Notice I emphasize *briefly* state your complaint. This is especially true for women. Most women (including myself) are not short on words, but truly one of the places in your life that you will benefit from being less descriptive is when you are complaining about what you don't like about your partner's ways. If you want a successful marriage, spend less time describing why things bother you. Instead, direct your emotional and mental energy into following these strategies and steps.

Look, I understand that sometimes you are going to have a bad day. The kind of day where your preschooler kept you up with an earache, you were late to work because you forgot to put gas in the car the night before, and your cell phone was going off repeatedly during an important meeting.

When you have a bad day, it is quite likely that you will be so frustrated that these relationship complaint steps may be the furthest thing from your mind. You may forget to follow the steps that will help your relationship complaints get resolved. When this happens, I hope your partner will improve his relationship service response by following the Relationship Repair Steps to servicing your complaint that will be outlined in chapters 5 and 6.

However, on your good days, your relationship will benefit if you are able to save the details when you are complaining. If possible, try not to elaborate on the numerous ways that your partner's inconsiderate behavior caused you a scheduling nightmare. I cannot emphasize enough how important it is to keep your complaint very, very brief. *In fact, try to say your complaint in two or three sentences. Then STOP!*

Let's give some a try:

- "I feel we are not giving our marriage enough attention. I don't think we have been out on a date just the two of us in several months!"

- "You purchased a new motorcycle? I feel you are not considering my needs when you buy expensive items without even discussing the purchase with me first."

- "I am really frustrated that you have been yelling at the kids more recently. I know you are stressed at work, but it is really affecting the mood of everyone in the family."

- "The situation with your parents and your brother is starting to get out of hand. You are talking about it a lot and are clearly upset, yet you keep avoiding having a discussion to confront the problem."

- "We have so many unfinished projects in the house. Whenever I bring up something we need to do, you get angry and I end up feeling like a nag."

- "Christine is getting some poor homework grades because it is not getting reviewed in the evenings. I feel there is too much on my plate now with the new baby, and I need more help."

Relationship Complaint Step #5: Tell your mate that you have a resolution in mind that you'd like to request. In this step you are continuing to be reasonable and calm. You are letting your significant other know that you have thought about this situation and that there is something she can do to help fix the problem. People generally like to fix problems and help their mates, so it is good if you can spell out what it is that you would like.

Now is the time to ask for the proposed resolution that you thought of back in step #1. If you are open to other possible resolutions, say that you will consider other possible ideas as well.

Hopefully, you are confident and able to ask for what you would like as a possible resolution, because you thought about it ahead of time and you believe that you are making a reasonable request. Remember that you are valuable and important. Also remember that you need to have your complaints serviced to maintain a happy, healthy relationship.

Some examples can show you what I mean:

- "Since our schedule has become more hectic with the kids and our jobs, will you work with me to discuss and identify times on the calendar when we can have date nights just for the two of us?"

- "In the future, will you tell me when you are thinking about making a purchase over $200 so we can discuss and agree on the purchase?"

- "Will you please talk with your parents about this problem and see if you can come to a solution so it does not keep bothering you?"

- "What would be the best way for us to plan household projects? Should we set aside time each weekend for a couple hours? Or perhaps we could both write down projects on a list in the kitchen and then agree on times to work on the projects?"

- "I know that yelling was not uncommon in your house growing up, but you know I am not used to it. Will you please keep working at not yelling at the kids?"

- "Can we change our agreement about who helps the children with homework? With a new baby in the house, I would like to know if you can review homework with Christine after dinner every night?"

Relationship Complaint Step #6: Finally, when your partner agrees to a resolution that you feel good about, say thank you and accept the resolution.

For example, if your mate apologizes, try saying, "I accept your apology." Too often people will continue to express their feelings and thoughts after they've already gotten an apology or received a resolution they've asked for.

I have observed people worrying or doubting themselves, "Did I ask for too much?" For example, there are times when I have observed women saying, "Maybe I'm being too hard on him." The same women then feel guilt-ridden and do not graciously accept the resolution that their spouse has just agreed to. However, I can guarantee that the same women would be far less guilt-ridden if the restaurant who messed up their order gave them a free dinner. Nor would these women be concerned about the profit margins of the store that gave them a refund for a defective hair dryer.

If you have a hard time saying thank you and accepting a positive resolution when your partner does something nice to fix your relationship concerns, then you are getting in the way of making your relationship successful. You are forgetting that you are valuable and important in your marriage, just as you are in your consumer/business relationships.

You bring certain qualities and strengths to the partnership, and it is important that you use your strengths to bring out the best in your partner. For example, if you are better at finances and budgeting, then it makes sense that you might occasionally file complaints about how your partner spends money. However, your complaints can help push your financial future as a couple in the right direction.

When your partner listens to you and agrees to give you the resolution that you asked for, take it and run with it! If you have a husband or a wife who will service and resolve some, if not most of your complaints, then count your lucky stars and enjoy your life. Instead of being guilt-ridden, try saying how much you appreciate that he takes your relationship seriously enough to resolve your concerns. You might also try to communicate to your significant other that their agreement to repair your concern helps you to trust the relationship even more.

So let's see how this interaction might sound with this example:

One of my clients, Kim, had a poor interaction with her boyfriend, Eric, about making plans for her birthday. We discussed that she became angry and complained about the boyfriend's inability to make her happy during special occasions. Eric shut down and withdrew, and my client was even thinking about not celebrating her birthday.

But on reflection, when we explored this situation, she really wanted to have a nice birthday celebration with him, and it would have definitely created more problems in the relationship if they did not have birthday plans. So we walked through the relationship complaint steps outlined in this chapter.

First, we discussed and identified a reasonable resolution since not celebrating her birthday without her boyfriend was, of course, not a solution that would make Kim happy. Kim decided instead that she wanted to ask Eric to show more enthusiasm during the planning for special occasions, including her upcoming birthday plans. (Step #1)

Then Kim thought of positive behaviors that her boyfriend has engaged in during birthdays and special occasions that she could thank him for. (Step #2) Kim decided to tell Eric thank you for often finding a thoughtful gift, one that really showed he listens to what she likes. When Kim thanked Eric for some of her past gifts, he seemed to relax more and was more open to her continuing to share her feelings.

Kim then opted to give her boyfriend the benefit of the doubt (Step #3) by acknowledging that she understood he could be struggling to be enthusiastic about special occasions due to some recent financial and work stressors. This stress was influencing Eric's ability to buy more expensive gifts, which is something he wanted to be able to provide her. Eric continued to be open to Kim when she was kindly giving him the benefit of the doubt.

Kim then practiced stating her complaint briefly, saying, "When we spoke the other night, it seemed to me that you were not very enthusiastic about making plans for next weekend for my birthday. It hurt my feelings." (Step #4) Because Kim kept the complaint brief, Eric showed understanding and he did not shut down and walk into another room.

Next, Kim asked for the resolution she identified earlier during step one. (Step #5). To her surprise, not only did Eric not shut down, he agreed to a resolution and the couple had a nice discussion about holidays and how to improve special occasions together as a couple.

Finally, when Kim came back in for her next session, she stated that it worked and Eric listened to her and showed more enthusiasm for the planning of her birthday. After her birthday, she thanked him for giving her the resolution she had hoped for. (Step #6) Ultimately, the couple had a lot of fun and Kim felt positive that she had avoided conflict over this situation. An added benefit was also that she was more confident that future events and special occasions would be more successful as well.

Relationship Complaint Step #1: Think about what would resolve your complaint before you make it.

Relationship Complaint Step #2: Start by saying something positive about your romantic relationship and your mate.

Relationship Complaint Step #3: Tell your partner that you are giving him or her the benefit of the doubt.

Relationship Complaint Step #4: *Briefly* state only one complaint in two to three sentences.

Relationship Complaint Step #5: Tell your mate that you have a resolution in mind that you'd like to request.

Relationship Complaint Step #6: Finally, when your partner agrees to a resolution that you feel good about, say thank you and accept the resolution.

Asking for Comfort from Your Mate

One of the things that people often joke about is that men from Mars like to fix problems while the women from Venus, on the other hand, just want to share their *feelings*. I am referring here to the Mars and Venus relationship disconnect between men and women proposed by author and counselor John Gray.

Women, when you are sharing feelings with the man in your life, he is likely to perceive that you are complaining—even if you are not complaining about him. Therefore, I recommend that you run through relationship complaint steps when you want to share your feelings or ask for comfort from your mate.

For example, maybe you are upset and want to complain to your husband about a disagreement you had with a friend. You believe that if you can talk and he listens to you for about five to ten minutes that you will feel better (You have identified a resolution, which is Relationship Complaint Step #1.) This complaint is not about your husband, so it seems as if you wouldn't need to follow steps 2 and 3. But if you can start out by telling him he is great (Relationship Complaint Step #2) and that you want to share your feelings, and that you have a complaint but is not at all about him (Relationship Complaint Step #3), then you are setting the stage to have him listen *and* you may even prevent him from drifting into defense mode.

Next, follow Relationship Complaint Step #4 and explain briefly, in fewer than two sentences, that you had a disagreement with your friend. Tell your husband that he can help resolve the concern you are having if he will listen to you for about five to ten minutes without giving you any advice (Relationship Complaint Step #5).

Now, you've just outlined how your husband can help resolve your *feelings*. He believes his role is to make you happy. In about twenty to thirty seconds he knows why you are emotional, that the complaint is not about him (whew!), and that his listening to you for a few minutes will help you feel better. This works. Your husband gets to fix the problem by listening to you, and you get to share your feelings. He just needs to understand that the way he can fix the problem is simply by listening to your feelings so that he knows exactly what his role is in the discussion.

Have you ever noticed that sometimes you start expressing emotions to your partner and you are seeking comfort but somehow it turns into a fight? Using the relationship complaint steps can help when you want to complain about something unrelated to the partnership that you are seeking comfort for.

When you are seeking comfort from your partner, instead of bursting into tears or starting to rant about your boss or your friend, try to start out by calmly asking for comfort using the relationship complaint steps.

When you want comfort from your mate, try to spell out exactly what kind of comfort resolution you want. In the previous example I just described, I suggested that you might ask him to listen to you for a few minutes until you feel better. But sometimes you may want a different kind of comfort, and I have offered some examples below. It is important that you learn what comforts you and then follow the complaint steps to ask for specific comfort.

If your spouse does not typically comfort you, then think about how you would like him to comfort you. Then, you can ask for the type of comfort response you would like the next time you are upset. What would make you feel better?

Here are some possible comforts you can ask for when you are seeking comfort from your mate:

- To hug you or to hold you while you are falling asleep
- To run the bath water for you
- To get you a glass of water or something to eat
- To go on a short walk with you
- To watch television with you, read to you from a book, or play a game of cards with you
- To rub your back or hold your hand
- To engage in reflective listening
- To give you advice or support about a problem

For many people, it is hard to ask for comfort. However, taking this step to ask for resolution in the form of asking for comfort when you are moody, upset, or sad will help your partner know what he can do to protect and care for you. Otherwise, if you are upset, emotional, or complaining and do not say how you would like to be comforted, then this may cause your partner to feel helpless. Helplessness breeds frustration and fighting. So asking for the comfort you need from your partner could ultimately prevent conflict from escalating.

Chapter 5

———•———

Step Right Up to the Relationship Repair Counter

Your committed relationship cannot be completely trusting, secure, and successful without a skilled Relationship Repair Counter. In other words, you should be constantly listening for the bell to ring at the repair counter. You will know the bell is ringing when

- Your significant other is upset, crying, angry, irritable, or moody and quiet.

- Your mate makes a complaint about your behavior (such as something you did or didn't do).

- Your partner complains about your character flaws or personality differences.

- Your spouse complains about other things unrelated to you or the relationship. For example, he complains about someone else's behaviors or character flaws (maybe his boss or business partner). (In this case, he is not asking you to service a complaint about your relationship. Rather, he is more likely looking for you to service him in the way of providing comfort, understanding, or advice.)

How would you grade your Relationship Repair Counter? More importantly, what grade would your mate give you? To give yourself a grade, answer the following yes or no questions:

- When your significant other is upset, do you start out by saying, "You are important to me, and I don't like to see you so upset"?

- When your partner is complaining (about your behavior or about something else), do you listen without interrupting?

- Do you regularly ask your mate, "What can I do to resolve this for you?" or "What can I do to comfort you?"

- Do you ask your spouse if you have made him feel better or if you have fully resolved her concern?

- When your significant other is upset, do you engage in reflective listening, such as saying, "So, your concern is [and restate the problem]? Is that right?"

If you answered yes to all five of these questions (and if your mate agrees), then you have an A+ in Relationship Repair skills. If you answered no to at least some of these questions, then you are likely missing some important steps that will help you have a more successful, secure romantic relationship.

In order to teach you steps for resolving your partner's concerns, I will be walking you through the steps that a business representative uses to resolve complaints. In order to effectively help couples learn to better resolve marriage and romantic relationship complaints, I have crafted Relationship Repair Steps from the recommendations of experts in business customer service. In this chapter, I will discuss how you can use these same steps in your romantic relationship to effectively resolve problems.

> **Relationship Repair Step #1: Tell your significant other that you value them and that you don't like seeing them unhappy.**

First, let's take a minute to think about how a properly trained customer service representative starts out addressing a complaint.

Customer Bob phones the customer service department at XYZ Appliances.

Maria (who has been well-trained at servicing customer complaints, answers the phone): "XYZ Appliances. This is Maria."

Bob: "The dishwasher we bought last month isn't working. I'm not happy about it. We paid a lot, and now it's broken already. We don't have time to wash dishes by hand." (A crying baby is heard in the background.)

Maria: "You are a valued customer here at XYZ Appliances, sir. May I ask your name?"

Bob: "Bob. Bob Smith."

Maria: "Bob, you are a valued customer here at XYZ Appliances, and we don't like seeing you dissatisfied. I sincerely apologize that you are going through this inconvenience today." (She is defusing her customer Bob's negative emotions.)

Bob: "Uh, yeah, okay."

Maria: "Let's see how we can help you today." Bob is surprised at Maria's response. He was half-expecting XYZ Appliances to drag their feet. In fact, he anticipated that he would probably get an automated response and that they wouldn't even have someone picking up the phone. When Maria picks up the phone and energetically tells him that he is a valued customer, his anger goes from a 10 down to a 4. He is glad to know that XYZ values him, and he feels that they are heading in the direction of resolving his concern.

Now let's imagine that Maria is not properly trained at servicing customer complaints. When Bob calls up (with his baby screaming in the background) and makes his angry complaint, Maria says, "You need to calm down and stop ranting at me. I didn't break your dishwasher. It's not my fault you are stressed out from having a new baby."

Now, Bob really has steam coming out of his ears, and he is ready to blow a gasket. He then proceeds to make other complaints and things escalate.

Bob explains to Maria: "XYZ Appliances could not fix our old dishwasher, so they sold me a new one. And I wasn't expecting to pay so much. On top of that, they took a week longer than the sales guy promised to install the new one. It was a huge inconvenience. Now, the new dishwasher, which I had to dip into my savings to buy, is broken.

Untrained Maria then says, "I'm not sure if we will be able to help you fix this. We'll have to send out a repair person. That's $100 for the service call and we can provide service on Tuesday between 8 and 12 or between 1 and 5. Which time works better for you?"

Now Bob is even angrier because the repair will cost money and he will have to take off work. Bob is fit to be tied over how inconvenient purchasing a product from XYZ Appliances has turned out to be. You can see the path this situation is taking, and it is not a smooth one.

Likewise, I have noticed that most conflicted couples fail to complete Relationship Repair Step #1 (tell your customer you value him). As a result, many couples end up on a bumpy road right from the start and conflict starts to escalate. For example, I observe both men and women mistakenly making comments such as these after their significant other files a complaint:

- "I am sorry you feel that way."
- "I think you are overreacting. I did not mean to do that."
- "Why are you yelling at me? I didn't do anything."
- "You are expecting me to get things perfect all the time. You are too critical."
- "I am working so hard. I just can't believe you think I'm not doing enough!"
- "It sounds to me like you are just ranting. When you can be calm and constructive, then come back and discuss this problem with me."
- "I was just teasing. You need to lighten up."

I believe it is unfortunate that people naturally respond this way, because most of my clients have great intentions. They absolutely want to have a happy life together, but they are not properly trained on how to create a secure relationship when it comes to resolving the complaints of their mate. Completing Relationship Repair Step #1 sets the tone for a caring, service-oriented discussion. You are basically telling your mate that you love and value him, that you want him to be happy and pleased, and that you desire to make things better. You have set the stage for properly repairing your partner's complaint.

I definitely recommend that you think of a thoughtful way to tell your mate that you value him. Here are some examples of ways to defuse your mate's emotions by telling him that you value him:

- "You are my number one. I hate seeing you upset, and I want to fix this problem so that you feel better."

- Quietly say, "I do not like seeing you upset, Sweetie. You mean a lot to me."

- "Honey, you are important to me, and I want to work this out with you."

- "You are a really good husband and father. I want to resolve this so that you are happy."

- "I am so thankful for how hard you work for our family. You are a great provider, and I feel just terrible that I disappointed you. How can I make this better?"

I am urging you to think about how you plan to communicate with your partner the fact that you value him. Why, you ask? Because, this is an extremely important step in the right direction. If you skip over this step or you don't do it well, then you are putting yourself at greater risk for an altercation.

Assuming that you don't like fighting, then I encourage you to make expressing value to your partner as second nature as checking your investment portfolio, planning your grocery list, or brushing your teeth. This is a *must do*. It is important to plan how you are going to communicate with your partner that you value him when he has a complaint.

> **Relationship Repair Step #2: Listen without interrupting while your spouse elaborates about his or her complaint.**

Relationship Repair Steps #2 and 3 are basically meant to assist you in going over your partner's complaint. I draw on the thinking of customer service experts Inghilleri and Solomon. The most important skill you can work on during this part of Relationship Repair is listening without interrupting.

Now, I am going to go back to our customer Bob and well-trained customer representative Maria. After defusing Bob's emotions, Maria says pleasantly to Bob, "Now, why don't you start by telling me more about what has been going on with your dishwasher."

After an effective customer service person addresses negative emotions by expressing the value of the customer, the next step is to say, "Will you tell me more about the problem that you are having?" Then, the customer service representative stops talking and listens patiently and does not interrupt. Sometimes, the representative may even allow the customer to complain and express various frustrations for several minutes.

If your spouse is mad at you, after you've completed Relationship Repair Step #1, I urge you to offer to listen to the problem. This positive action is an example of what is called "turning toward." It involves showing that you are open, willing to listen, and primed for a discussion about the problem, according to work by the Gottmans and colleague DeClaire.

For example, you can say

- "I hope you will share with me what is on your mind. I'm ready to listen."

- "Will you tell me all the reasons that you are mad at me so I can understand?"

- "Please tell me more about the things that are bothering you."

- "I will listen to your feelings about what I did to upset you so that you can get this off your chest."

This step may be one of the most difficult for most couples. Why? Quite often, the partner who is complaining exaggerates some of what she is saying because she is emotional. It is also likely that her complaint is sprinkled with other frustrations or stressors. As a result, it is difficult to listen without interrupting to correct the exaggerations and inaccuracies.

For example, think of customer Bob who is upset not only about his broken appliance, he also had a bad day at work, has a headache from seasonal allergies, and don't forget the baby crying in the background. So, while he is complaining, he wrongly states that XYZ Appliances was a week late delivering the dishwasher (even though it was actually four days late, not a week).

Fortunately, Maria overlooks the exaggeration and focuses on the overall message that Bob is irritated about slow service in the first place and the current situation, which is the broken dishwasher. She is looking at Bob's account and can see that the dishwasher install was actually a few days late instead of a week, but she does not interrupt to correct him.

Can you imagine if Maria had said, "Bob, you are a liar. You are telling me that it took seven days, and I can see here on your account that it was actually only four days."

Instead, she listens to the overall message that Bob feels that he received slow service as a first inconvenience, and that he now he has a broken appliance as a second inconvenience.

It is difficult and certainly an act of "service and honor" to your relationship if you are able to overlook some of the exaggerations and frustrations expressed by your mate. Try to listen for the overall message of what your wife is telling you.

During this step, I highly recommend that you do not interrupt or correct the accuracy of your mate's statements—even if she is exaggerating or does not have all the facts straight. Instead, focus on hearing what the overall complaint is. Filter out and put aside any inaccuracies or exaggerations that your spouse says. Stripping the emotions from the complaint and focusing on what is true and understandable about the complaint will often assist you in moving toward stabilizing the conversation.

While your mate is talking, I understand that sometimes it can be tempting to search for a mute button in order to avoid the noise. However, I want you to do the exact opposite and instead really listen so well that you can basically repeat back what your partner is saying to you. It is important to listen to everything your spouse says so that you can pass the knowledge check at the end of the conversation.

When she says, "Honey, you weren't listening to a thing I was saying," I want you to be able to say, "Yes, I was listening. And I understand. What I am hearing you say is [*restatement*]."

After your partner is finished speaking and there has been a pause, move to Relationship Repair Step #3.

> ## Relationship Repair Step #3: Conduct reflective listening, "What I am hearing you say is [*restatement*]."

The excellent customer service representative, after listening to an upset customer (who might even be yelling), will calmly say, "What I'm hearing you say is [*restatement*]."

For example, Maria might say to customer Bob, "Okay, what I am hearing is that you are really unhappy that this dishwasher broke and you are now being inconvenienced, especially after you were inconvenienced waiting for the dishwasher to be delivered and installed. Is this right?"

Bob then says yes. He feels Maria understands him. He also feels relieved because he was able to complain and get everything off his chest. His anger and emotions are now down to a 2. Because Maria has defused the emotions, Bob is now able to focus on negotiating a resolution with XYZ Appliances.

In a romantic relationship, the temptation after your spouse has been complaining is to either correct her on one of her exaggerations or to tell her a solution to the problem. However, it is likely that she is still emotional or even angry, so if you want to negotiate a resolution, it is important that you complete Relationship Repair Step #3. Using reflective listening will continue to defuse negative emotions and will let your mate know that you acknowledge and fully understand her complaint. Reflective listening further sets the stage for proper repair of the relationship problem.

There are different ways to conduct reflective listening. One of the most common methods is to say, "What I am hearing you say is [*restatement*] in your own words. Did I get this right?" This is my therapy technique. I say this repeatedly during every therapy session because I want to teach and role model how to do reflective listening, which is a key relationship skill.

Here are some other possible phrases you can use to engage in reflective listening:

- "It seems that what you want me to understand is [*restatement*]. Is this right?"

- "If I understand you correctly, the message you are trying to communicate is [*restatement*]. Am I correct?"

- "So, your concern is [*restatement*]. Am I getting this right?"

I recommend that you come up with your own phrase that you use for reflective listening, such as "What I am hearing is…". Make your reflective listening response your mantra. Practice using it with your coworkers, with your customers, with your friends, and with your kids. Then when your partner is mad at you (one of the most difficult times to remember to do reflective listening), it will be habitual for you to say, "Oh, what I'm hearing you say is [*restatement*]. Did I get this right?"

If you get it right, you will see your mate's body language start to change. Her frustration is being soothed as she hears you repeat back to her the message she wants you to understand.

Even if you do not understand the message correctly when you restate it back, most of the time your spouse will feel better that you are trying to understand. She will be able to see that you are trying to listen to her. However, when your significant other says, "No, you're not getting it," the best thing is to ask her to explain what you missed so that you can try again. Sometimes you may have to try two, three, or four times before you fully understand your spouse's complaint.

Keep trying to say, "So, your concern is [*restatement*]. Am I getting this right?" until your mate says yes. Until you hear yes, you have not finished this step. When you do, then you can move to Relationship Repair Step #4.

> ## Relationship Repair Step #4: Ask what will resolve your partner's concern.

Imagine Bob complaining to Maria at XYZ Appliances, and she says, "Bob, I tell you what I am going to do. I am going to send you another copy of the instruction manual so you can figure out how to repair your dishwasher. We are too busy selling appliances over here at XYZ."

What? Bob is thinking, *You didn't even ask me what I wanted for a resolution!* The response that might come out of Bob's mouth next could make some people's ears bleed. A new copy of the instructional manual was not what Bob had in mind to resolve his problem.

Fortunately, most business service representatives like Maria are trained to say, "Bob, what can I do to resolve your concern?"

However, you might be surprised how rare it is for couples to ask this question of each other. My observation is that husbands often jump to fixing the problem by saying, "I know. I will do [*his solution*]." The wife, on the other hand, becomes furious because her husband's offer to fix the problem is not what she wanted for a resolution. The husband's attempt to fix the problem with his own solution equates to XYZ saying they will send out a new instruction manual, which is not the resolution that Bob was looking for.

Again, there is some good intent to fix a problem, but the rush to resolution is damaging. Look, if you tell your partner how you are going to fix the problem, your heart is headed in the right direction. You are earnestly attempting to make your wife happy. But you are not doing it in the best way. If you want to please your significant other, instead try asking, "What will resolve this for you?"

This can be asked in a variety of ways, such as

- "Baby, what can I say or do to resolve this concern for you?"

- "What can I say or do to make you feel better?"

- "Honey, is there something I can say or do to comfort you, besides listening?"

- "Do you have any ideas about what I can say or do that would fix this for you?"

- "Are you able to tell me what you think would resolve this for you?"

- "Well, I really made a mistake, what can I do to make it up to you?"

Asking "What will resolve this for you?" is an extremely powerful question, but ideally it will be asked after you've done the previous steps, which all take care of defusing the other person's emotions—and set the stage for negotiating a resolution.

If you do not remember the other steps, sincerely asking the question, "What can I do to resolve this for you?" is the most powerful statement that you can make during an argument with your partner.

There is a good chance your spouse may not have taken the time to identify what resolution she is ideally looking for. Asking this question helps her to start thinking in the direction of resolution. Or, if your spouse has unfairly assumed that you don't care about resolving the matter, then asking "What will resolve this for you?" will hopefully change her mind.

I can tell you that even though I teach these steps, and I believe in them, occasionally I revert to a bad habit that most of us humans have.

A couple in my private practice will start to tell me about a problem they are having, but they have not stated a resolution. In a few cases, I have made the mistake of beginning to suggest a possible resolution. If the solution is not what my clients have in mind, then they sometimes look annoyed and can even become more agitated. (Often, couples are already agitated when they are coming to couples therapy—as you can imagine).

I am sometimes surprised to learn that what my client had in mind was a resolution I had not even considered! (And believe me, I have a toolbox full of resolutions). So this is an important lesson: always ask someone who is filing a complaint what they think is the ideal resolution *for them.*

Meet Terry and Troy

I will never forget a couple that I worked with who had been married for about twenty years! Terry was disappointed with her husband because he was not listening to her; however, he said he was very happily married and he had no complaints about his wife. I assure you that I remember this couple so well, because this almost never happens!

Usually both people start couples therapy each with their own list of unresolved complaints. In this case, the wife was also unusual because did not have a long list of complaints. Rather, she had only one complaint: her husband should talk with her more.

I kept suggesting different possible resolutions such as phone calls during the day and date nights but she liked none of my ideas. I was forgetting to follow my own advice!

Finally, I asked her how her husband could resolve her complaint. She needed time to think about it, but she decided she would like her husband to take a walk with her every evening after dinner to talk about her day and for him to talk about his day. I asked him if he could do this. He said yes.

The couple came back a few weeks later, and the wife was now perfectly happy in her marriage. This one resolution had fixed years of her complaining that he was not listening to her.

Of course, not all of my couples have such a breezy time resolving a problem in therapy, but I can honestly say that asking the question about resolution usually changes the tone. This step starts to shift the conversation toward a resolution. If your spouse does not have any answers for the resolution, you can give her some time to think about it. Or if you have a suggestion about how to resolve the issue, you can say, "I have a suggestion. Can I tell you what it is?"

Some possible resolutions that are the most common in romantic relationships are these:

- An apology

- A new agreement that prevents the same problem from happening in the future

- Words of reassurance about anything that might make your partner feel better

- An acknowledgement that you understand her perspective

- Some action that makes your partner feel important in order to "make up for" or overcome a previous mistake that you made in the relationship (Think of a restaurant manager giving you free appetizers and drinks because they messed up your dinner order.)

- An agreement to receive help from a professional or an outside source regarding a problem that you are having (For example, if there is a financial problem, you might agree to see a financial consultant.)

One of my favorite options for resolution is to suggest that you will do something to make up for a mistake. For example, you can offer to take your sweetie out on a date or massage his shoulders as a way to make up for a problem you may have caused, even if it was not purposeful.

You have now essentially entered the negotiations for a resolution. Sometimes resolution comes quickly. Ideally, your partner will suggest a resolution that you think is reasonable. You quickly agree and the problem is solved. Being open to compromise can drastically change the way you and your partner handle conflict.

At other times, the negotiation process can take some time and energy. If you start to get impatient while you are going through negotiations, I recommend that you think about how much time and energy it consumes to quarrel without reaching resolution.

I like to tell my clients that I do not think anyone should be a doormat. You should not always have to accept every resolution your partner proposes right away. If there is some reason that you disagree with the proposed resolution, then I want you to explain to your significant other why you feel that way. Then, I would like you to suggest to your partner that you want to compromise and negotiate a different resolution.

> ## Relationship Repair Step #5: Negotiate
> ## a resolution with your partner.

Try to imagine Bob asking Maria for a fully paid vacation because his dishwasher is broken. Of course, Maria is undoubtedly not authorized to give out vacation packages in exchange for broken dishwashers.

If the customer is asking for an unreasonable resolution, then the business service representative will usually negotiate with some alternative suggestions for resolution. For example, Maria might offer Bob a repair person to fix the dishwasher within twenty-four hours at no cost to him. Or she might offer to give him a new dishwasher, with installation, at no cost. Because of the inconvenience, she might also offer to give him a gift card or a small refund on his original purchase to make up for the defective product and the days of washing dishes by hand.

Likewise, it is possible that your mate will sometimes ask for a resolution that you think is either unreasonable or something you cannot agree to. What do you do if your spouse wants the sun, and the moon, and the stars?

If this happens, start with the positive and again remind your partner that you want to resolve her concern, but you are unable to provide the specific resolution she is requesting. At this point, it is a good idea to think of one or more reasonable resolutions or possible compromises to offer your partner. Hopefully, he or she will accept your offer and you will agree on a resolution even though it may take more than one offer to resolve the matter.

If you follow all of the steps and you think that your spouse is repeatedly and regularly unreasonable (problems do not get resolved as a result), then you may start to wonder if you are the unreasonable partner in the relationship. In this case, you can seek professional advice from a marriage or family expert as to whether you are being reasonable or not. Or you might ask a couple of trusted friends their opinion.

I offer a service via my private practice in which I conduct relationship coaching via phone or videoconference. For a small fee, you can describe your situation in a fifteen-minute, thirty-minute, or forty-five-minute coaching session. One of my associates or I will give you an expert opinion on the matter. You might explore similar options with therapists in your area.

What should you do if you keep offering various suggestions for resolution, and your mate does not like any of them? Additionally, your mate has not offered any resolution. Just let her know that you want to resolve the matter. Ask your partner to think of suggestions for resolution, then to revisit the Relationship Repair Counter.

If the problem still does not get resolved, I would suggest that you take it seriously. You may want to consider Relationship Repair coaching or a session of couples therapy in order to resolve the problem. Not resolving a problem, especially one that you keep having conflict about repeatedly, leads to an insecure relationship that is headed down a collision course.

> **Relationship Repair Step #6: Ask your mate if you have fully resolved the concern.**

After customer Bob and business representative Maria have agreed upon a resolution (Bob took Maria's offer to send out a repair person the next day and receive a gift card), Maria asks Bob, "Have I resolved all your concerns? Is there anything else I can do for you today?"

Trained service representatives are taught to ask the customer this at the very end of the conversation. They are taught to not assume that the customer's complaint has been fully resolved until they have asked the questions and heard the customer say that he is completely satisfied with the resolution.

When the business representative takes a moment to make sure that the complaint is fully resolved, the customer again feels valued and satisfied with the transaction. Typically, the customer will continue conducting business with this company. That is, even though the business made a mistake or there was a problem in the business relationship, trust has been restored and the business relationship continues. All businesses make mistakes. It is how businesses rectify the situation that truly differentiates one business from another.

Similarly, in a personal relationship, I highly recommend that you ask your significant other, "Do you feel better? Have I resolved your concern? Is it okay if we start dinner now?" Asking your spouse if the complaint has been resolved seals the deal. It makes your spouse feel special, secure, and satisfied. Although you made a mistake or there was a problem, trust and security have been restored and the romantic relationship can resume.

Relationship Repair Step #1: Tell your significant other that you value them and that you don't like seeing them unhappy.

Relationship Repair Step #2: Listen without interrupting while your spouse elaborates about his or her complaint.

Relationship Repair Step #3: Conduct reflective listening, "What I am hearing you say is [*restatement*]."

Relationship Repair Step #4: Ask what will resolve your partner's concern.

Relationship Repair Step #5: Negotiate a resolution with your partner.

Relationship Repair Step #6: Ask your mate if you have fully resolved the concern.

Some of the complaints that you receive at the Relationship Repair Counter will likely be the result of "perpetual issues"— those that continue to arise because of differences in personality or perspective. In fact, research at the Gottman Institute has found that 69 percent of marital problems can be classified as "never ending" or better known as "perpetual issues."

According to the Gottman Institute, finding some sort of resolution (even if the resolution is simply agreeing to respect that you have a different point of view), can help two people with personality differences still have a satisfying relationship based on trust and security. Coming to a resolution sends the message that you value and respect your spouse, which makes it easier to accept each other's differences.

Furthermore, in a business setting, it is always a good idea to proactively follow up a few days or weeks later. Successful business representatives will often follow up with their customers. They check in (now often by email survey) to make sure the customer is satisfied with the follow-through on the resolution.

They ask the customer: "Do you think that we are doing what we said we were going to do to resolve your concern?"

In your romantic relationship, I recommend that you do the same thing. A few days or a couple weeks after you have resolved one of your partner's concerns, ask: "From your perspective, do you think I have followed-through on our new agreement?"

Chapter 6

———— ◆ ————

Whatever Happens, No Matter What,
Please Do Not Jump Over the Relationship Repair Counter

Jim walks up to the customer service desk at his local cable company.

Jim: "My cable box is not working right. You need to replace it. I missed the Nebraska football game Saturday."

Jane, the cable customer service representative, pulls up Jim's account. Then Jane jumps over the customer service desk and says, "Yeah, well you were late on a payment two months ago."

Jane is now making her own complaint and both Jane and Jim are on the same side of the customer service counter. No one is servicing anyone else's complaint.

Whoa, didn't see that coming, did you?

The customer service counter has basically lost its identity and has completely shut down. The result is that no one's complaints will be heard and no resolutions will be made. Now, Jim, the customer, is furious because he knows for a fact that Jane could care less that he missed watching the football game on his only day off. He makes a sarcastic comment to Jane and pretty soon they are both bickering.

Someone watching this interaction might not even be sure who the customer is or who registered the complaint. Furthermore, as things continue to escalate, Jim is also likely to be thinking about changing cable companies.

This is a rather ridiculous example to point out how ineffective it is to file a complaint in response to a complaint.

Believe it or not, even though it sounds silly hearing about this kind of response within a business context, a scenario just like this plays out with troubled couples who are having conflict on a regular basis. Meet Susan and Jeremy.

Susan: "I really do not understand why you did not call to tell me you were going to be two hours late. I could have left to do an errand or went ahead to the party on my own. Instead, I was sitting here worried about you, and I kept wondering where you were. That is just so rude!"

Jeremy: "Well, you're not so perfect yourself. Just last week you showed up late to Mom's house." (Jeremy has now jumped over the service counter, and he is filing his own complaint.)

Susan: "Are you kidding me? I was only like ten minutes late, and I called you. This is not even the same thing. You were two hours late, and the point is that you didn't call me. I want you to promise me in the future, that you will call me."

Jeremy: "I'm not going to promise anything to someone who shows up late for things."

In this example, one partner (Susan) files a complaint, and the other (Jeremy) reacts *defensively.* Responding to your spouse's complaint with your own complaint or by defending yourself is called defensiveness. The Gottman Institute has identified defensiveness as one of the "Four Horsemen of the Apocalypse" because it has the potential to escalate in ways that are a strong predictor for divorce.

In my opinion, it is often difficult for people to get a handle on how defensiveness is operating in their own personal relationships. So I have created the metaphor of jumping over the customer service desk or the Relationship Repair Counter, if you will. The problem here is that both people are hanging out in front of the service counter bickering. No one is staying behind the Relationship Repair Counter long enough to resolve any complaints. Nothing gets resolved, so the conflict can go on for minutes or hours or days, depending upon the couple.

If you want a happy relationship with a loved one, when your significant other complains, I am recommending the following: In all circumstances, NO MATTER WHAT, please refrain from jumping over the Relationship Repair Counter. Stay behind the service counter and service your partner's complaint.

This means that when your spouse makes a complaint, you will have to stop yourself from thinking about your own complaints in the relationship.

Take a minute and think about how you normally react when your partner makes complaints. These are some common examples of *unhelpful* thoughts that people sometimes have when their significant other makes a complaint:

- "I can't believe she is complaining. I am a much more helpful husband than Mary's husband."

- "Do I have to get everything right? I do this right. I do that right. Now I make a mistake, and I have to deal with him picking on me. Pick, pick, pick."

- "What the heck? I was mad at her on Tuesday. I just didn't say anything about it because I was trying to be the bigger person. Now I'm really going to let her have it."

- "If he wants to start a fight about money, no problem. I can fight about the kids anytime because he is never around. He can bring it on."

Of course, these thoughts are not conducive to the Relationship Repair Attitudes that I introduced in chapter 3, and these kinds of negative thoughts tend to lead to the following defensive reactions:

- Comparing yourself to someone who is behaving worse. This is deflecting the attention off you and onto someone else. In this case, you are actually jumping over the Relationship Repair Counter and filing your own complaint that your mate is not being appreciative.

- Complaining that your spouse is being too critical because you do so many things right. In this case, you are also jumping over the Relationship Repair Counter and filing a complaint that your mate is overly critical.

- Complaining about a behavior that you do not like about your partner. Just like Jane and Jeremy did in the previous examples, you are shifting the focus to a different topic or complaint that you have. In this case, you are jumping over the counter and shifting the focus on your own concerns rather than servicing your partner's complaint.

In all of these cases, I urge you to consider if you would have these reactions in a business or work context. Most likely not. From my work as an employee assistance counselor and consultant, defensive reactions are less frequent in the workplace although at times they are still a problem. Furthermore, I would note that conflict usually escalates in the workplace when there is defensiveness.

In all honesty, I think jumping over the Relationship Repair Counter is human nature, which is why many couples end up with so much conflict. When your partner starts to complain about you and something you did wrong, it is naturally going to trigger thoughts about your own unresolved relationship concerns.

A scenario that often occurs in busy families is the following: You have an occurrence in which you and your spouse do not see eye to eye on something (let's say, your spouse is overspending at Target), but the timing is not right for you to complain. Maybe you are in public and get an overdraft alert on your checking account when you view your smartphone messages. Or perhaps you are eating dinner with your in-laws. Or maybe you are both right in the middle of the routine to get your preschooler and toddler to bed.

So you don't ring the Relationship Repair bell. By the time you get home or get the kids in bed, you have focused your attention on something else (hopefully something more pleasant), and you still have not communicated your complaint. Eventually, something will happen that will trigger your spouse to have a complaint, and she will bring her complaint to the Relationship Repair Counter. Suddenly, any and possibly all complaints that you had in the back of your mind are now on the tip of your tongue. If your mate is going to complain, then so are you!

But the fact of the matter is this: if you want a secure and trusting relationship, then there can only be one person on the side of the counter who is making the complaint. The other person has to stay on the serving side of the counter to handle the complaint.

For example, when your husband starts to complain that he thinks you spent too much money on back-to-school shopping for the kids and you find yourself thinking about how he spent too much money on his golf game over the summer, you must put that thought aside and revisit it later. He made the complaint about the school supplies budget, so it is important to respectfully find a resolution for that concern. Then, if the entertainment budget and the cost of golf is a concern that you have, by all means you can now bring your complaint to the Relationship Repair Counter.

In all fairness, I recommend that if your spouse brings up a relationship complaint, please service that complaint first—all the way from Relationship Repair Step #1 (Tell your significant other that you value them and that you don't like seeing them unhappy) through Relationship Repair Step #6 (Ask your mate if you have fully resolved the concern).

Only then, after you have completed the repair steps, can you then ask your spouse to reverse roles by asking your partner to repair a complaint that you have. You might say this: "I am really glad that we worked this out. Now I am wondering if your Relationship Repair Counter is open to discuss a concern that I have." If you notice that your partner is regularly jumping over the Relationship Repair Counter when you ring the bell, you might want to think about your timing. There are several strategies in the next chapter that you can implement in order to reduce defensiveness. However, one of the most important is timing.

Sometimes you may attempt to go to the Relationship Repair Counter when your significant other is at work (via the phone, text, or email), in public, or in front of the kids. In these cases, you are not likely to get a receptive response because in reality your partner cannot effectively handle your complaint while at work, while making decisions on what kind of produce to get at the market, or while juggling your children's needs. These are times when the Relationship Service Counter is definitely closed.

I recommend that you wait until it is a good time and your partner can readily sit behind the counter and properly handle your complaint.

Meet Janelle and Mark

Early in my career, Janelle and Mark came to marriage counseling because of ongoing conflict and fights. Mark's main complaint: Janelle was constantly calling him during the day while he was working his corporate job. His company had given him a Blackberry, and he was always available.

Janelle was angry that he was "always available" to his numerous corporate contacts but not available to her. Whenever she filed her complaint that Mark was not giving her or their children enough time and attention, he jumped over the Relationship Repair Counter or he walked away. Janelle, not unlike most

American consumers, was quite persistent about finding out when the Relationship Repair Counter was going to be open and when Mark was going to finally service her complaint.

The intervention was twofold. First, Mark was taught to recognize that Janelle was going to keep ringing the bell, quite literally driving him nuts, as long as he continued to not have his Relationship Repair Counter open. Just like customers will keep calling the customer service number, or stand at the service counter to get their complaints serviced, Janelle was quite convinced that she should be treated with value in her marriage relationship.

Second, Mark resolved Janelle's complaint by opening his Relationship Repair Counter during the therapy session. He committed to taking Janelle out on two date nights every month and taking time every Saturday afternoon for a family outing. Janelle was pleased as punch and the bell stopped ringing. Mark was able to focus at work for the first time in weeks, so he learned the benefit of opening his Relationship Repair Counter during his time at home.

Since 2003, I have seen many couples with similar problems. The intent of my interventions is to resolve the most pressing complaints a couple has when they first come to my

Relationship Repair shop, and it is also to teach the couple how to have a Relationship Repair Counter, how to effectively register and service complaints, and how to find the right timing to repair typical relationship problems.

Sometimes people jump over the Relationship Repair Counter because they are less in tune with relationship problems than their spouse. In other words, a man is generally not really thinking about relationship problems (or his relationship for that matter) until the woman in his life starts to complain about a relationship problem.

For example, most women are socialized to spend more time thinking about family and personal relationships; whereas, most men are socialized to think more about competition and being a good provider at work. So it makes sense that women bring up more complaints about romantic and family relationships than men. However, I have noticed that when women complain, the men suddenly tune into the relationship channel. A man does not feel good about his woman filing complaints, and he feels helpless to know what to do and the result is that he panics and becomes defensive. He then jumps over the customer service counter and makes his complaints known as well.

I am confident about giving the next advice to men. Here is some news that may help you. If the woman in your life brings up more complaints than you do, you do not need to compete with her. It is not a competition to see who can come up with more complaints. Such an environment will create more defensiveness. Counterattacking or attempting to defend yourself by jumping at the chance to criticize the person with the complaint will not help if you are both still in the business of maintaining and strengthening your relationship. The "bring it on" attitude resolves nothing.

If she complains about you more than you complain about her, it does not mean that you are a less worthy partner, less wonderful, or less special. It simply means that she probably naturally shifts to thinking about the marriage relationship more often than you do, and therefore she is going to have more complaints. For example, women are more likely to spend time studying how-to and self-help books (like this one), magazine articles, and blogs to inform themselves on how to have a successful family life.

Men, if you service her complaints, she will feel satisfied and secure. If you have complaints that you forgot about because you are more inclined to focus your attention on the NFL or the stock market, then by all means bring up your complaints after you have finished resolving hers. But if you don't have any complaints about her, don't try to create one just to show her that you are equally as good as she.

Most women do not bring up complaints to be better than their husbands. Some men feel that when the woman bring up a complaint, that this is a power move, but really it is not. Most women bring up complaints because they have a concern they feel is legitimate, and they want it resolved. In fact, women feel they can be closer and more intimate with a partner who resolves concerns. Many women—want to feel valued at the Relationship Repair Counter so they can proceed with their shopping. They want the relationship to continue forward in a positive way.

Chapter 7

—◆—

Ring the Bell for Relationship Repair Strategies

> **Repair Strategy #1: Tell Your Partner Often That You Want to Make Him Happy, and Remind Him to Bring His Complaints to You.**

Have you ever noticed that many stores' customer service signs used to be small and the counters were tucked away in the back corner of the store? Nowadays, when you walk into a business, you will often see the customer service sign right in the front.

Many stores have changed the accessibility of the customer service counter, and one reason for the increased visibility is to invite customers to bring complaints when they have them. A second reason is because businesses want to make it more convenient for customers to get complaints serviced. The business realizes that if a customer is coming to the customer service counter, that buyer may already be inconvenienced. The business does not want the customer to search for the customer service counter at the back of the store, because this will likely add to the customer's frustration and escalate the problem.

Likewise, I encourage you to make relationship service easy for your mate. Remind him often that your Relationship Repair Counter is available to take complaints. In other words, flash the Relationship Repair sign often during the start of spending time together. In addition, some of the following strategies can help to make the servicing of complaints more convenient for your mate.

Repair Strategy #2: Plan the Hours When Your Relationship Repair Counter Will Be Open

---

People sometimes complain that their partner brings up complaints at very poor times such as at night when they are trying to go to sleep. You know what I am talking about— the kind of conversations that can seriously lead to sleep deprivation. I have also had numerous clients during my years providing marriage therapy who complained that their mate would call them with relationship complaints while they were at work.

When counseling with these couples, I quickly identified that one of the partners with a pressing complaint did not know when her mate's repair counter was going to be open. So the frustration grew and they just kept trying to ring the Relationship Repair bell to see if it was open, even while their mate was at work.

While conducting marriage counseling, I have noticed that some couples are not only fighting about parenting, money, or sex, but in some cases couples start fighting about *when* to work out problems! Of course, one of the best ways to prevent fighting is to have your partner trust that you have a regularly open and skilled Relationship Repair Counter.

Try this: when your significant other comes to you in order to have a complaint serviced, even if it is an inconvenient time, stop and resolve the complaint via Relationship Repair Steps from chapter 5. Ask what will resolve your mate's concern. After you have successfully resolved your partner's complaint, you have now developed greater trust in the relationship. Your partner trusts you to service complaints, so now she is more likely to wait for your Relationship Repair Counter to be open in the future.

**Tell your partner when your Relationship
Repair Counter is open to receive complaints.**

Most disgruntled people, whether spouses or consumers, can wait for the service counter to open, if only they know when it will happen. Businesses are accustomed to conveying to consumers when their customer service department is open because they recognize that this is an important part of a trusting relationship.

Likewise, your committed relationship will benefit if, for example, you tell your partner that you can best service complaints between 8 and 10 p.m. (after the kids are in bed but before you are too tired to discuss the matter). I have learned that my husband, who is a corporate sales manager, services complaints best on Saturday or Sunday afternoons when he is well rested, has had time to exercise, and is not in the middle of servicing his customers. He has figured out that I do not do anything well in the morning, including repairing marriage complaints.

I recommend that you primarily attempt to repair relationship complaints when you are in a good position to do so. Sometimes a business person will be tempted to take an adversarial call from a disgruntled client even when she is not really in a position to be able to address the customer's concern. At that moment, it is important for the business person to make a decision on whether the timing is right to take a call. I am not saying to dismiss the customer. What I am saying is that sometimes it may be better to wait just a little while until you are positioned properly with additional facts and energy to address the situation.

Furthermore, with businesses requiring their employees to multitask, it is a smart move to make sure that business customer service associates can give disgruntled customers their undivided attention. If a disgruntled customer leaves a message asking an account representative to return the call, sometimes it is better to wait. Preparing mentally and practically to be able to provide positive conflict resolution is a smart move.

Inside of romantic relationships, you may be servicing complaints while trying to multitask paying bills, completing chores, and giving the children attention. However, I recommend that you choose times to open your Relationship Repair Counter when you are not stressed or multitasking.

For example, it is good to choose a time of day when you are not too tired, hungry, or distracted. There is an acronym known as HALT that mental health professionals frequently use in addictions counseling. HALT reminds addicts who are in recovery to stop and take a break when they are Hungry, Angry, Lonely, or Tired. I think HALT also applies to servicing and making marriage complaints. If you or your mate is hungry, angry, lonely, or tired, it is not the most ideal time for a marriage meeting to bring up and service complaints. Some complaints cannot wait and need to be resolved right away, but in many cases you can learn to wait to discuss problems at an ideal time.

You and your partner will both benefit from knowing when your Relationship Repair Counter is open. However, if your mate rings the Relationship Repair bell outside of the regular service hours that you have identified, then I would suggest that you still service the complaint if at all possible. For example, when a crisis or other unplanned event happens, I recommend that you try to respond quickly. The more prompt you are at taking care of problems, the sooner you regain a trusting and secure relationship that is more pleasurable, happy, and fulfilling.

In some cases, your significant other may have a complaint regarding when your Relationship Service Counter is open or closed. If this happens, then you may consider resolving that complaint by adjusting your Relationship Repair hours to a mutually agreeable time. Keep in mind that it is important for you to identify a time that is good for both you and your partner. Otherwise, when she complains, it might remind you of fingernails on a chalkboard. Imagine a business telling you that the customer service department is only open between 3 and 5 a.m. Or that the only time they are open is between 3 and 5 p.m. when you have to pick up the kids from school, drive them to activities, and then cook dinner.

Quite simply, it would be extremely inconvenient, if not impossible, for you to go to that business's customer service counter. You just might start conducting your business elsewhere.

Similarly, it is important for your romantic relationship that you negotiate times that are good for you *and* your partner when the Relationship Repair Counter will be open. Servicing and properly repairing complaints is work—it is not the fun, pleasurable part of your relationship—and it takes time, so try to pick a time when it is convenient and comfortable for both you and your mate.

Businesses, by and large, have really improved by giving the customer some idea of when they will be servicing a complaint. For example, now when you call customer service, you are often told how long you will have to wait or how many people are ahead of you in line. Businesses have become smarter in this way.

In the corporate world, customers who have registered a complaint via email will often get a reply telling them what the timeline is for getting a response. Generally, people like to know a business has received their complaint and that the business has a time scheduled to address it. Ultimately, this instills a sense of security in customers.

Communicating with your spouse regarding when your service counter will be open or what timeline works for addressing his complaint is a good idea. When you give your partner a timeline, you are essentially giving him a carrot, something to hold on to. Then, as long as you follow through with actually servicing the complaint within this timeline, you can delay the Relationship Repair until a more convenient time while still helping your partner to grow trust in the Relationship Repair process.

Repair Strategy #3: Put the Relationship Repair Bell on the Counter

Sometimes a customer is sending signals to a salesperson that she is not happy. For example, the customer might be sighing and repeatedly checking her watch while waiting. Or she might be rolling her eyes or tapping her foot. The salesperson, however, is not picking up the vibe. Instead, he may be too focused on closing the next deal or on building a social relationship with the customer. However, successful businesses make a point of having a customer service bell at their counter—in addition to having a specific phone number and procedures for customers to make complaints.

When I observe couples, I notice that sometimes one person is expressing a message of annoyance to the other—meaning she has a significant complaint. But somehow the other person is not registering it in his mind as, *This is a complaint that I need to repair.* As a result, the partner fails to take the proper steps and soon a small problem has developed into a catastrophe.

I recommend that you put out a Relationship Repair bell at your counter. Of course, I do not mean a real bell, I mean a symbolic bell. To do this, partners should help each other choose a method for alerting the other when one is seeking to repair a complaint.

I have asked many couples to do this in counseling, and each couple has come up with their own strategy. For example, one couple I was working with would say, "Not to start a fight, but …" Using these words was their way of letting the other person know one partner was ringing the bell and she was now standing in front of the Relationship Repair Counter.

Another couple I saw in counseling liked the customer service metaphor so much that they started saying, "Is the customer service counter open right now? I have a complaint."

I can honestly say that sometimes I am guilty of not noticing when my husband is registering his complaint at the Relationship Repair Counter. Sometimes Brendan will be expressing his thoughts about something, and I can see that it bothers him, but it does not register in my mind that his concern rises to the level of being a relationship complaint that is so serious it needs to be repaired. Obviously, I am alert to repairing relationship complaints since I am writing a book about it. I say this to make the point that I do this for a living, and sometimes I still do not recognize that my partner is trying to register a complaint.

This is why it is so important for couples to identify what words will be the Relationship Repair bell to signal that communication is needed. Decide on what word, phrase, or a signal will be the "bell" in your relationship. Then, I definitely recommend that you pay attention and provide good customer service when you hear the service bell ring because this is essential to having a successful relationship.

Repair Strategy #4: Complete Regular Research about Your Mate

Besides providing prompt and friendly customer service, you will notice that a good business invests in research and development regarding the products and services that appeal to their customers. And they don't stop conducting research after they attract a customer. The consumer research is ongoing as the needs and wishes of their customers change with time.

Likewise, let me suggest that it is important to regularly engage in research to figure out what your significant other likes, and you must remember that there are likely to be some changes over time as your relationship develops. Pay attention to the following: What does he wish for? What does she say that she hopes for? When he is angry, what does he complain about and how can you fix it? Are there needs that your partner has that you are not meeting? Ask your mate what services you engage in during the relationship that she likes and continue those services. Ask your spouse what services he wishes you provided that you either forget to do or need to learn. Develop yourself in such a way that you are pleasing to your mate.

I cannot stress this enough. Often, one part of a relationship can be powerful enough to attract a mate. For example, a woman may be attracted to and marry a man who is a wonderful provider and emotionally steady. However, if her overall needs and wishes are not researched, developed, and provided for, her new husband may have trouble keeping her as a mate. After marriage, it may be necessary for the husband to also engage in romantic gestures to make the marriage work even though this is not what initially attracted the woman to select him as a partner.

After completing research, praise your partner for the things that are most important to her *and to you*. If a supervisor tells an employee that she likes what he is doing, it often motivates that employee to do things more routinely and possibly even improves his procedures. The same is true in your romantic relationship. Notice, appreciate, and praise what you like about your partner. Complimenting your significant other will likely motivate your partner to make the behaviors you like more routine and habitual.

Repair Strategy #5: Plan Times for Regular Meetings

Successful businesses have regular budget meetings, planning meetings, review meetings, and retreats for team-building. At these meetings, there is a purpose or an agenda stated at the beginning. The meeting stays focused on the purpose and the agenda.

If you want a successful partnership with your mate, then the same should be true for your relationship conversations. If you want to have a conversation with your partner, try telling him what the purpose of the conversation is at the beginning. If the purpose is to have fun and connect after a long day, explain that your agenda is to connect and enjoy each other's company. Does he agree with the agenda? Since women often initiate conversations and meetings, I urge you to get your husband's agreement on the agenda ahead of time. You are far more likely to have a successful discussion or transaction with your mate when you do this.

I recommend that you plan times for regular meetings in your marriage as well. Dr. Curtis, author of *The Business of Love*, also recommends budget meetings, review meetings, and planning meetings and retreats for a couple's relationship. I also encourage you to have weekly or monthly planning meetings. Discuss what is on the calendar, who is responsible for what tasks, and how you will accomplish your goals.

During planning meetings, you can also check up on any emotional concerns your partner may be having. Frequent meetings are opportunities to give feedback to your partner about previous agreements you have made regarding responsibilities, budget, and other issues. During these meetings, start with the positive and show appreciation. Then discuss any concerns you may have.

Repair Strategy #6: Scratch Each Other's Backs

That's right. You've most likely participated in the business philosophy of "you scratch my back, and I'll scratch yours" or you've possibly seen it in the movies. Either way, the idea is a good one in business relationships. It refers to a mutual contract in which both people obtain what they want from the other person.

Given the current high divorce rate, it seems as if maybe we need to do a little more mutual spousal back scratching. Give it a try! When your partner makes a complaint, this is actually the perfect opportunity for you to figure out where and how he wants his back scratched. Once you figure it out, by all means do the scratching.

Unfortunately, I have noted that some people have had poor role modeling when it comes to back scratching in marriage. For example, in our grandparents' generation, if a husband did not scratch his wife's back, there was not a whole lot she could do about it. Because of this, there are many people who have not had proper role modeling. In other words, they have not seen their parents and grandparents engaging in mutual back scratching as a couple. The problem here is that these same people may not recognize that the consequence of not engaging in mutual back scratching could lead to divorce nowadays. The majority of today's couples, men and women, are looking for a mutual contract and a mutual partnership.

For example, if your wife went with you to the football game, which is not really her favorite thing to do, then she thinks she is scratching your back. Next month, when she asks you to go to the ballet, she is likely to get angry if you say "no way!" Look, I get it that the ballet might not be your favorite thing to do; however, I recommend that it is only fair for you to scratch her back, which means going to the ballet, because she scratched yours (and, no, you don't have to wear a tutu).

In business, this concept of mutual back scratching is also sometimes referred to as a win-win. In win-win relationships, both sides put on the table their priority needs. Ideally, they negotiate an agreement and a relationship that benefits the priority needs of both parties. Our definition of a win-win does not necessarily mean that either party in the business relationship obtains everything they want. To the contrary, win-win is a result that occurs when both parties are effectively able to negotiate an agreement that they feel will mutually benefit their organizations.

Let's go back to the football and ballet example. In some relationships, I have observed that when a spouse requests to go on a date to the ballet or to watch a football game, their mate says no. Perhaps because I am so intent on the business concept of back scratching, I am usually shocked to observe one mate denying the other's request outright.

In this example, imagine that a husband says, "But honey, you *know* I don't like going to the ballet." His wife then starts complaining about how she doesn't really like football, but she goes with him to the local pub to watch football with his friends and their wives. I have observed, in some cases, the husband again saying, "But, honey, you know I don't like going to the ballet." The problem here is that this husband is missing the point—he is not recognizing the importance of back scratching.

I vividly remember a couple in marriage therapy where the husband complained that his wife would not watch the Steelers football games with him. This really angered him because he loved football. He commented that his friends' wives put on their jerseys and put out popcorn and nachos and watched the game with their husbands. He had decided this was important to him in his marriage. He was a hard worker and took his wife to church on Sundays and helped her with household chores. Churchgoing was more her deal than his, but he attended almost every weekend with her.

Furthermore, he helped her with household chores every weekend to free up time to watch the game. He felt strongly that he was scratching her back, and he was indignant that she would not scratch his. She would say, "But, baby, you know that football is not my thing."

With this couple, I encouraged the wife to negotiate times to watch football games with her husband each season. In business contracts and relationships, the fact is that there is always a mutually beneficial contract that includes back scratching.

According to marriage research, generally women are more likely to compromise or be influenced by what their husbands want. Men, on the other hand, can sometimes feel threatened by compromise because it feels as if they will be relinquishing some of their power in the relationship.

To the contrary, the ability to come to a compromise can raise the amount of power, respect, and appreciation the husband has in his romantic relationship, according to the Gottmans' research. I like to encourage men, who generally have a lot of strengths within business relationships, to think of the concept of win-win and back scratching to help them see the possible benefits of compromising as a way to earn greater respect, power, and appreciation in the business world. Likewise, the same is true in the world of marriage.

Some people are telling themselves that a romantic relationship does not include a mutually beneficial contract. However, this same person is taking a huge risk for potential failure. It's possible that your partner might continue to stay and scratch your back even if you don't scratch his. However, if you love your partner and want to keep the relationship, this is a gamble you might not want to take.

Sadly, I have witnessed some partners who unknowingly gambled away their marriage. Basically, they did not service their partner's complaints, did not complete relationship research, and did not scratch their partner's back. They came in for counseling *after* their husband or wife had already moved out and moved on. They want to know what to do differently in their next relationship so that they have success as opposed to divorce.

There are no guarantees, but if you notice during courtship that your partner takes care of your complaints and if you notice that you can generally service your partner's complaints and resolve them, then you have the beginning of a trusting, secure relationship that can work through problems and conflict.

If you haven't been together long enough to figure that out, then I would suggest not going into a partnership with that person until you do. I assume you wouldn't commit to doing business at the same location for the next fifty years without knowing if that business has a good customer service department complete with excellent back scratching. Likewise, it is never a good idea to commit to a romantic relationship for the next fifty years until you have great trust in your partner's relationship service and back-scratching ability.

In the next chapter, I address more about Relationship Repair during dating and courtship.

Chapter 8

———— ◆ ————

Try Before You Buy: Relationship Repair During Dating

Dating is the perfect opportunity to practice having a Relationship Repair Counter, especially during the time when you are dating one person exclusively. Whether you are male or female, and no matter how old you are, developing a Relationship Repair Counter to fix problems in a dating relationship is vital. People who are dating have to be able to repair problems that inevitably come up in order to continue having a fun and secure dating relationship.

Dating is the perfect opportunity to find out if someone you like has a Relationship Repair Counter.

Sooner or later, the person you are dating is going to do something that you do not like. Hopefully, if you think your date is super good looking and you love their personality, the first date will be perfect. But, eventually, anybody that you date is going to do something to hurt your feelings. The question is what to do about it.

Should you break up with them? Some people get very freaked out as soon as the dating relationship encounters a problem. If the problem is a deal breaker for you, then you should break off the relationship, but a lot of problems people encounter during dating are not deal breakers.

For example, if you have decided that someone having any kind of history of drugs or alcohol addiction is a deal breaker for you and you find out that the person you are dating is drinking excessively, then that is a deal breaker for you. I would not suggest that you compromise your overall values.

However, if you find out that your boyfriend ignored you on a Friday night to stay home and play video games, you could try to file a complaint and see what happens. For example, in this case you could say, "You know, I really do not want to be in a dating relationship with someone who values video games on Friday night over having a date night. I really would like to have an agreement that you will take me out on Friday nights, and you will save your video games for week nights. What do you think?"

I personally tried out the concept of filing pertinent relationship complaints during my dating life. Like most women, inevitably, no matter who I dated there was no shortage of ways that men could disappoint me. I remember very well on a third or fourth date with my husband, he was cursing. (Not at me, of course, or that would have been a deal breaker!)

Brendan sells buildings to general contractors in the construction industry and the men talk like sailors. So I clearly remember stating something to the effect that, "I am a lady, and I really don't like you cursing around me like I am one of the guys you work with."

I clarified the resolution I was seeking was not that he would never curse, but that I reasonably felt that most of the time in conversations with me or in future family situations with children around he would not curse. I do not hold myself to the standard of not cursing when I stub my toe or get stuck in traffic, so I was clearly not asking for a no cursing policy. I just wanted to not be in the construction zone.

I was pleasantly surprised that Brendan had a Relationship Repair Department. I actually do not remember exactly what he said, but I do remember that his behavior changed when we spent time together, and I noticed he was not cursing except infrequently. I recall that he acknowledged that he had gotten into a bad habit, and that he understood why I wanted him to make that change.

Now, this may seem like a small change for someone to make. No big deal. But contrast that with my other reasonable requests from some of the previous men that I had dated—and the response was a refreshing change. In Brendan I had found someone I could work with! I felt he valued me enough to make the change; whereas, for example, I had asked another man I dated to slow down his driving and he instead went faster *and* laughed. His Relationship Repair Counter was not open for numerous complaints, so I ended the dating relationship.

Another funny story is that Brendan teased me about a rather large purse I had when we were first dating. The first problem was that this showed his lack of fashion sense, since big purses were in style at the time. If he were to tease me now about my purse being too big, I would probably just laugh but for some reason on that particular day it really rubbed me the wrong way. I filed a complaint, and he has never said anything negative about any of my purses, whether large or small, for years. Now that is some real romantic relationship service for you, right?

How someone you are dating responds to your complaints is something for you to pay attention to. Even if you are dating someone with no consideration of marriage, it is simply less frustrating and healthier to date people who will value you enough to respond to reasonable complaints that you make. Someone who will not give you a resolution to any of your complaints is typically a highly defensive person with more controlling characteristics. Run away as fast as you can!

No one is perfect, so please keep in mind that your date might not always respond well right away. The Relationship Repair Counter might not be open at the moment. For example, you might have surprised your date with a complaint when he was getting tired or hungry. Or she may need to sharpen her complaint resolution skills. However, the items to pay attention to are these:

- Does the person you are dating make at least some of the changes you have requested?

- When you file a complaint are you eventually able to get to a resolution or a compromise, even if the process takes some time?

- Does your dating partner then follow through with resolutions that he has agreed to?

Perhaps you are dating someone really wonderful, except that she does not respond well to complaints. Trust me when I tell you that the unresolved complaints will likely grow until your dating partner is not so wonderful or likeable. In this case, if you really like this woman, then I would suggest that you start filing complaints about your dating partner's ineffective Relationship Repair Counter. You might try telling your girlfriend that you have noticed a pattern that she regularly dismisses and ignores your concerns.

Ultimately, if the person cannot learn to respond to complaints and honor at last some of your requested resolutions, then I hope you will value yourself enough to break off that dating relationship. Your dating partner certainly does not value you if she will not honor resolutions to your complaints and concerns. Someone who values you in a romantic relationship does more than kiss and hug you, take you out to the movies, and cook dinner for you. Please remember that someone who values you will do the hard work and the service involved in having an effective Relationship Repair Counter.

If you are with someone who never resolves your complaints in his actions and behavior, my advice is to run! This is not someone you can share a home with, work with, love, marry, or have as a helpmate in a long-term partnership.

In fact, if you are with someone who does not resolve reasonable complaints that you make, I hope you will talk with friends or a professional therapist to verify that your complaints are reasonable and normal. Chances are your concerns are normal, and I hope you quite literally will break off this kind of unhealthy relationship because a mentally healthy person will absolutely resolve at least some of your reasonable complaints.

Meet Carrie and Nathan

One example of a dating relationship that I assisted with was when Carrie came to relationship therapy with a boyfriend Nathan whom she was considering getting married to. Carrie was thirty-two, and she wanted to get married, settle down, and have children. Her boyfriend, thirty-one, wanted the same thing, and the couple had discussed a future proposal.

The couple had numerous strengths, but Carrie was disappointed that Nathan was not more validating toward her. Instead of complimenting her, Nathan frequently teased Carrie. We explored that Nathan's family was not very close, that he was much more comfortable with teasing than with compliments.

Carrie gave specific examples of ways that Nathan teased her that she did not like, and he agreed to stop most of the teasing (not all) and to start praising Carrie more and giving her genuine compliments.

Several weeks later, Carrie was beaming at a follow-up appointment because Nathan had changed his teasing to compliments. She explained that because he changed his behavior, she ultimately felt he was more tender and kind to her, which was more in line with what she wanted in a husband and father. Even more important, Carrie had become more confident that Nathan valued her enough to make changes that were important to her, solidifying that he has a Relationship Repair Counter necessary for a long-term committed relationship.

Meet William and Erin

In another example, William came to a session because he was concerned that Erin, his fiancée, was talking with two of her former boyfriends behind his back. Erin explained that she only spoke to them infrequently on the phone and that she did not think it was any big deal.

She was defensive, complaining that William was being controlling and jealous, that she did not do anything wrong and that she would never cheat on him by going out with these guys or sleeping with them. The couple went through several fights over this problem before showing up at my office.

William complained that he was worried that Erin was not being honest with him. When I asked the couple more about this situation, Erin admitted that William had not directly accused her of cheating on him. William agreed that he did not think Erin had cheated on him in terms of meeting up with her former boyfriends. However, he was concerned that Erin did not tell him that she still spoke to them on the phone occasionally.

With this couple, I helped Erin to open her Relationship Repair Counter and to tell William that she valued him. She listened to him talk about his fears that a phone call could lead to something else, but more importantly he wanted to trust her. The couple discussed two possible resolutions, but they ultimately decided that they would not talk with ex-boyfriends or ex-girlfriends without telling each other, "Hey, I spoke with so and so today." They also agreed to tell each other if someone were to pursue them for a meet-up or romantic encounter.

Please keep in mind here that I have worked with other couples who come to other resolutions about this same kind of issue. For example, I have worked with couples who do not ever talk with ex-boyfriends or ex-girlfriends as a general rule of thumb for their relationship. The point is that Erin was able to find a resolution that helped William feel that she valued him and that she cared about resolving his complaint. The couple was able to get past the discussion about cheating, accusations, and jealousy by remembering to ask the simple question, "How can I resolve your concern?"

Dating is not only an opportunity to see how the other person responds to complaints and problems, it is also your opportunity to practice sharpening the skills for your own Relationship Repair Counter. After you are dating someone exclusively, explain to your girlfriend or boyfriend that you know that you will make mistakes but that you want to work out problems and mistakes in your relationship.

Try to keep your antennas up for anything that seems like a complaint. When it happens, remember to practice the steps from chapter 5 about how to respond to a relationship complaint.

The most important thing is to remember to ask the person you are dating what you can do resolve their concern or how you can help to make the problem better. If you are dating someone whom you value, I urge you to think of many different ways that you can ask the question, "How can I resolve this complaint?"

After all, you don't want to sound like a customer service representative at a store. I do recommend, however, that you figure out how to repair relationship complaints. And remember, the only way to really know what someone wants is to ask.

Chapter 9

———◆———

What If Nobody Listens? Breaking Cycles of Helplessness

If you have failed in your romantic relationships in the past or if you have concerns that your current relationship is failing, I would urge you to think about whether you are creating a situation in which your partner feels helpless. On the other hand, perhaps you service your partner's complaints, but you feel helpless in getting your concerns serviced by your partner.

There are many ways to hold power over someone else and to make them feel helpless or small. One way is to beat someone up physically. Another way is to deny someone things she needs to survive, such as money for basic necessities or to keep her from friends, creating isolation. Finally, another way is to dismiss and ignore someone's important and reasonable concerns over and over again.

I realize that if you have not been repairing your mate's complaints properly, there is a good chance that your intention was not to cause feelings of helplessness or to hold power over her. However, that is exactly what you are doing. Although many people may not think of it in this way, I want to call attention to a very important key factor in romantic relationships: If you are not regularly servicing and repairing many of your partner's complaints, then you likely are causing the person that you love to feel helpless. Causing helplessness in this way is a sure way to inflict mental and emotional abuse on your partner.

In many cases, you are the only person to whom your mate can turn to have certain needs met. If you choose not to service many of your partner's complaints and give him the desires of his heart, you are holding power over him. You are likely participating in causing your partner to feel small, helpless, and unimportant, which may have the same kinds of long-term mental health effects as physical battering.

The long-term effects of not resolving many of your spouse's complaints are your spouse suffering from feelings of insecurity, fear, anxiety, confusion, and helplessness. Having helpless feelings on a regular basis within a committed relationship can contribute to your partner having depression, panic disorder, tearfulness, irritability and anger, substance use and abuse or other addictions, distrust of you and others, infidelities, and divorce.

On the other hand, having an effective Relationship Repair Counter will decrease feelings of helplessness for couples and in families generally because children learn role modeling from their parents. It is so important that we step up our game when it comes to having a Relationship Repair Counter, because diminished feelings of helplessness within family relationships reduces risks for mental health disorders, teenage defiance, substance abuse and addictions, and criminal behavior. Our society will benefit from good examples at the Relationship Repair Counter within committed relationships.

If you don't believe me, then just think about trying to do business where you can't get a complaint serviced. How do you feel when the business refuses to service your complaint even after several attempts?

- Do you feel valuable or do you feel unimportant? Likely you feel unimportant. The more times you have tried to get your complaint serviced, the more unimportant you believe you are to the business.

- Do you feel frustrated and angry? Most likely, the longer you wait for your complaint to be serviced, the more angry and frustrated you become.

- Do you trust the business will honor you or do you start wondering if they are cheating you in some other kind of way? I believe it is normal to question a business's overall agenda when you are not serviced correctly or in a timely fashion.

- Do you want to continue this business relationship or do you think about conducting business somewhere else?

When you promised to love and honor your mate, you were also promising to serve her at the Relationship Repair Counter, whether you understood that at the time or not. You were promising to take care of her—that means that you are responsible for making sure that you do not make her feel helpless on a regular basis. This means you will honor and repair most of your mate's reasonable complaints.

Of course, I believe it may be impossible for a person to acknowledge and service all complaints right away. Similarly, no business can immediately service all complaints nor can any human being. However, it is reasonable to expect your partner to value you enough to service your complaints the majority of the time with a Relationship Repair Counter that is regularly open.

Here is what amazes me. A whole lot of well-meaning, spiritual, good people have amazing intentions for their marriage, but they are unintentionally psychologically harming their spouses because they do not have a functioning, skilled Relationship Repair Counter.

The scenarios and steps in chapters 2 through 7 may not seem that challenging at first glance. But putting them into practice is very difficult. We sometimes find it hard to have humility, to listen patiently, to behave kindly, and to serve our family members and our partner.

When you use the Relationship Repair techniques to effectively service your partner's complaints, not only are you refraining from mentally battering him and creating helplessness, you are doing the exact opposite. You create a respectful, caring relationship—a close bond. Your partner feels that you value him. He trusts that you are in this together and willing to fix problems. He can see that you are humble and unselfish.

In my opinion, we need a new way to go about having healthy, committed relationships. Although the expectation to stay married still exists, the norm has changed drastically in the past fifty years with much higher levels of divorce, and in essence one of the main reasons for divorce is that people do not have an effective Relationship Repair Counter.

I think that many Americans have a fix-it attitude of service and humility. Many of us are simply falling short of applying this attitude to our romantic, committed relationships. I believe that Relationship Repair can fill some of that gap and give couples the necessary additional skill sets and behaviors for today's marriage. From my observation, couples are regularly going to the Relationship Repair Counter complaining for mutually contractual partnerships. So we need the business skill sets to take care of those complaints.

Ironically, the skill sets that are required in romantic relationships are of course not just business-minded; the attitudes and skills needed at the Relationship Repair Counter are spiritual because they require humility, service, patience, and kindness. Also, by modeling Relationship Repair behaviors, intimate partners can teach their children within families an example of relationship service that helps to break intergenerational cycles of violence and control within our families.

Relationship service modeled within marriage and family will give children and adults the practice they need to be more productive workers and employees, as well as healthier and more respectful family members and lifelong romantic partners.

What to Do If Your Partner Does Not Have a Relationship Repair Counter

If your mate does not have a Relationship Repair Counter, you cannot force her to have one. This likely makes you feel helpless, frustrated, devalued, and hurt. Quite literally, you may even feel mentally beaten down after you make a complaint and your partner becomes defensive.

You can keep making complaints and requests for different service. However, ultimately, if your significant other refuses to make adjustments, you will have to decide whether you can live under these conditions: not being valued and feelings of helplessness are important concerns to get resolved. In these cases, you may have to think about how serious your unresolved relationship concerns are and how important they are to your quality of life.

In some cases, if your spouse does not effectively resolve your concerns, I would suggest that you try to role model going through the Relationship Repair Steps and servicing your spouse's complaints. If you have not been doing a great job repairing your spouse's complaints, then being the first to change this within your romantic relationship will likely breed more security.

By trying to follow the Relationship Repair strategies and concepts yourself, you are basically role modeling the kind of reaction you would like when you register a relationship complaint—then you can ask your mate to repeat the same process when you make a complaint.

If you have been role modeling for months or years, and your partner still does not learn to have a Relationship Repair Counter, my heart goes out to you. It really does. You are likely feeling beaten down and helpless, and you are most likely experiencing some symptoms of depression and anxiety.

In this case, you will likely have to evaluate how damaging your feelings of helplessness are to your overall mental and physical health. Many of my clients over the years have come to my private practice to try to confront complaints that have gone unresolved for a long time with their mate. Often times, people even have thoughts of ending a long-term committed relationship if they do not finally get resolution to a long-standing complaint or concern. I encourage people to take the following steps before ending a relationship.

Ring the alarm bell. Tell your mate that you are feeling so devalued and helpless about the complaint that you have thoughts of divorce or ending the relationship if the complaint is not serviced properly.

Be persistent about your complaint. Keep filing it and asking for the resolution that you would like without backing down. Sometimes having the support of a therapist during this process is extremely helpful. When people confront long-standing unresolved complaints, there is usually a very strong resistance from their partner to make changes. Family systems do not change readily or effectively in some cases. You may have to withstand days or even weeks of conflict to finally get the resolution that you think is just and fair.

Finally, as a last resort, in some cases I have observed that if someone tells their partner, "If this does not change I am going to have to discuss it with someone outside the relationship to get some perspective." You can then suggest that you will tell a therapist, a pastor, a mutual friend, a family member. I have seen countless times when this kind of confrontation changes behavior. If your spouse will not resolve reasonable complaints with reasonable behavior, sometimes the suggestion that you will talk with others about it is enough to get that person thinking about what others would say. In some cases, I have seen people go so far as to then tell other people about the problem after they have rang the alarm bell and still there is no change. This strategy causes enough pressure to create change and resolution in the relationship.

After trying all of the strategies above, if your partner still will not resolve reasonable complaints *and* if your complaints become too great—you may opt to end the relationship that you have invested so much time and energy into. This will naturally be very painful for you, but please keep in mind it has also been painful to continue relating to a mate who continuously causes you to feel helpless. I hope you will know that you have value and seek future personal friendships and possibly a future romantic partner who values you enough to have an effective Relationship Repair Counter.

Chapter 10

———— ♦ ————

Problem Solved: The Joy of Success
at the Relationship Repair Counter

I want you to know the joy *and* the profitability of Relationship Repair success. If you have not known what to do when your partner is complaining about a relationship problem, then I believe that following the repair steps in this book will inspire and help you.

So many people—men and women—have come to my office with feelings of helplessness. The wife is upset, but the husband doesn't know what steps to take to fix it. The husband is angry, but she has no idea where to go next. People want to save the relationships they have invested in, but they keep saying the wrong things and soon their significant other is just *more upset and angry.* Yikes!

All too often, I witness both women and men saying all kinds of *unhelpful* things at the start of Relationship Repair therapy. For example, when their spouse files a complaint in my office, they give excuses instead of focusing on resolution. These same people have great intentions of service and love for their family, and by the time we are finishing up a few sessions, these couples are often on a much better path.

I imagine the same for you, and I want you to know the joy of Relationship Repair success. Although it takes humility, work, and skill to service your partner's complaints, I trust that you know the joy and success that comes from a job well done and the gratification of achievement in another part of your life such as:

- You are confident at work. You are part of an organization that provides an important service or product to others.

- You are a wonderful, attentive mother to your children and your home. People tell you that you are a fantastic homemaker.

- You successfully service and resolve the problems of your customers. Customers write letters of praise to your boss regarding your service.

- You proudly and unselfishly serve your country or your community in the military, law enforcement, or fire and rescue. Saving and protecting lives is gratifying.

- You heal and teach people via service as a health care provider or you serve as an educator. You love educating our youth.

- You generously serve your community as a volunteer or minister in your church community. You create a sense of peace in people who are searching for hope and a faith in God.

- You own a business that provides a service to consumers. You watch your business and your profits grow.

Whether you are successful in one of these roles or another that I did not mention, it is likely that you have had at least some (if not extensive) training along with a thorough review of policies and procedures. Or you have taken the time to read and educate yourself about how to best parent your new baby or how to minister to your church.

As a result, you feel competent and confident in yourself. You work hard and when you do a good job, you get compliments from your supervisor and coworkers, along with promotions, higher pay or profits, and respect from colleagues and friends. I certainly hope you realize these joys.

Yet even if you have the joys of a job well done in your business, work, civic, or parenting life, you may not have the joy of knowing what profits will ever come from your having a joyful, successful committed relationship if you do not properly service your partner's complaints.

As I said, servicing the complaints of your mate requires work, humility, skill, and dedication. However, just like in your business and vocational life, if you apply Relationship Repair principles, you can have numerous profits and successes. I urge you to try the steps in this Relationship Repair program for six months to one year. Demonstrate to your partner that you will service complaints and notice how your relationship blossoms, how your partner changes, and how gratifying it can be.

Some likely profits from your hard work at servicing relationship complaints may consist of one or more of the following results:

- A happier spouse who feels that you value him or her

- A calmer, more secure mate

- Less fighting between you and your partner

- Your significant other having fewer feelings of helplessness, anger, and sadness
- Your partner learning to better resolve your complaints via your example
- Your spouse bragging to friends and family about how good your marriage is
- Better teamwork in your relationship as you learn to make adjustments that your partner suggests
- A better sex life with your mate
- Your children witnessing more respect and less fighting
- A more productive mate at work and in the household
- Decreased risk of infidelities and divorce
- Decreased risk for mental health symptoms and substance use problems for yourself, your partner, and your children
- More personal development and skills (because your spouse will likely complain about your weaknesses and character flaws and thus lead the way to your self-improvement)
- Breaking the cycle of helplessness within intimate relationships

If I have not already inspired you to change your responses to your partner's complaints, then I hope that this list will motivate you.

Sometimes people say in marriage that "the two shall become one." When two people commit to each other, they agree to be each other's helpmates, team partner, and back scratcher. If you have made this kind of commitment, the only way you can truly be a team with your significant other is if you are influenced by your partner and make adjustments for and with your mate. Sometimes pride gets in the way, and although you might know that your spouse is right, you may be reluctant to say, "Okay, I will work on changing that about myself."

The only way you can truly be a helpmate is if you make adjustments for your spouse. When your mate has certain reasonable expectations that you know would make your life together better, then you ought to make those changes. A team has to be correcting in order to be effective. If you want to be married and have a significant other in your life, responding to complaints and making changes is an absolute requirement! If you commit to a romantic partner, it means you will have to allow yourself to be openly influenced by your mate if you want a successful long-term relationship. Your mate is helping you change and grow those parts of yourself that need adjusting. Often people say, "If you love me, then you shouldn't try to change me. You should accept me for who I am." I am challenging this thinking when it comes to romantic relationships.

Just like it is important to have balance in other areas of your life, it is also important to strike a balance between accepting your mate but also gently asking your partner to correct and improve their weaknesses.

It is important to allow your partner to help guide you toward improving your personal weaknesses. We cannot help but be influenced by certain qualities of the person whom we have chosen as a mate. So it's good to accept that person's help, including their prodding to diminish certain weaknesses that might get in the way of practical, financial, family, and relationship goals.

I understand that sometimes your partner registers a complaint, trying to help you with a weakness. But it is not the kind of "help" you were asking for, right? I get it. For example, Larry complained that his relationship would benefit from a night without the children every couple of weeks. However, Leslie described that she was having a terrible time feeling guilty about leaving the two-year-old kicking and screaming with the babysitter. In this example, Leslie was convinced she did not need "help" from Larry. But he was insistent that the couple needed to get out without the children.

Larry persistently complained for months, finally calling my office, stating that although he appreciated that Leslie is a devoted mother, she was giving too much attention to the children and not enough to the marriage. In this case, Leslie finally conceded and after a couple times of leaving the screaming toddler behind, she acknowledged that Larry was right. The date nights were good for the marriage in the long term; whereas the tantrums were short-lived.

It is important to recognize when your spouse's complaints are legitimate. By doing so, you are accepting the help you most likely need. If only you are humble enough to hear your partner's complaints and make adjustments accordingly, then you will become a more complete person and a better partner. Additionally, if you find thoughtful ways to express complaints to your partner and to ask for adjustments, your mate can become a more complete person by learning from your strengths.

The bottom line for your romantic relationship is this: if you service your partner's complaints, you are more likely to have relationship, financial, and overall personal success.

Meet Peter and Francesca

I would like to give you two examples of positive outcomes from Relationship Repair. I recall meeting with Peter and Francesca. Peter ran a small, but highly profitable business. His wife focused her attention on their home and children. The husband had few complaints about the marriage. His wife, on the other hand, was dissatisfied and was threatening to file for divorce if her husband did not make some adjustments.

During this first session, we clarified the two concerns she had were her husband's yelling at her and the kids, to the point of cursing and being out of control, and his spending too much time at work. As she started to discuss her concerns, her husband became defensive and tried to explain the reasons for his behaviors. However, he was not proactively servicing and resolving his wife's complaints. The couple was stuck in a vicious cycle of the wife regularly complaining about the same problem, the husband becoming defensive, and the couple not reaching any resolution.

In this case, I was easily able to ask the husband how he responded to complaints in his business. I then helped him respond the same way to his wife's complaints during the marriage counseling sessions via Relationship Repair Steps outlined in chapter 5. Within three sessions, this couple was finished with treatment and to my knowledge are doing well.

Some couples may spend more than three sessions in marriage therapy if they have more concerns than the couple described in this example. In fact, an average is six to eight sessions. Furthermore, the Relationship Repair approach is not meant for every couple. Rather, it is an approach that can be used to help couples who are struggling with conflict resolution. Some couples may be in treatment for various other issues, such as one person may be struggling with depression or post-traumatic stress disorder, the couple may be seeking sex therapy for a problem in the sexual relationship, the couple may need help after one partner has had addictions treatment, or a couple may seek assistance with how to parent their children.

Meet Mike and Elaine

Mike and Elaine started marriage therapy in a crisis because Mike had gotten so fed up that he threatened to end the marriage. Elaine was shocked and surprised to find that Mike was nearly ready to throw in the towel. She had no idea because he never complained or challenged her ideas for years. The couple rarely had conflict in the past—Mike had been conflict avoidant.

I can still vividly remember Mike explaining to me that the children were now teens and that Elaine had a history of getting angry and controlling the decisions in the family for over a decade. Mike said he was not able to give his opinions or share his thoughts because it might cause Elaine to get angry. His main complaint was the frequency and intensity of her anger.

Fortunately, Elaine was willing to open her Relationship Repair Counter, and she acknowledged that Mike had a valid complaint. She clarified what changes she would need to make in order to resolve the complaint. Most important, Mike simply wanted Elaine to learn to share her thoughts and feelings without getting angry. He also wanted her to learn to accept that he may have different opinions and to listen to him without getting angry.

We did some work by looking at Elaine's controlling behaviors, which came from her family of origin. She worked at making the requested changes. After about six sessions, Mike said he wished that he had spoken up sooner because he was much more satisfied in his marriage. We did some work on his history of conflict avoidance and how he developed avoidance as a coping mechanism. Mike recommitted to Elaine, and the couple was able to save their marriage.

Having a Relationship Repair Counter has also been a blessing to my own marriage. It has been both fun and helpful for my husband and me to discuss and work on the concepts of Relationship Repair together. Brendan helped me with an early draft of these concepts, in a first book that we called *MarriageBiz*. By incorporating business ideas with our personal experiences, we hope to both inspire and help other couples and also better resolve our own differences.

I can honestly say that sometimes when my husband and I are having a relationship disagreement, we remind each other the steps we are supposed to be taking to resolve the problem—so we can get back to having fun. The customer service concepts in *Relationship Repair for Couples* help us to better remember what the next step is in servicing our own marriage complaints.

I am confident that this book can change some of your general attitudes about relationship complaints. I hope you now can see how your partner's complaints can help you grow personally, help you build trust and loyalty in your romantic relationship, and improve your teamwork. I trust that you can now see relationship complaints in a more positive light rather than negative.

I promise you that with a Relationship Repair Counter you will have less drama and more success in your romantic relationship. Specifically, I trust that Relationship Repair will become a constructive tool for servicing your partner's complaints. I urge you to be as ambitious about your marriage and home life as you are about your work and your financial life. Both your business and personal life are intricately intertwined, and I hope that having a Relationship Repair

Counter will be a symbol for you of just how much your work life and your personal life are tied together.

Now, let's roll up our sleeves and get to work providing excellent Relationship Repair. I can hear that service bell ringing now!

References

Curtis, John. (2006). *The Business of Love: 9 Best Practices for Improving the Bottom Line of Your Relationship.* IOD Press.

Gottman, J., Gottman, J. S., and DeClaire, J. (2006). *10 Lessons to Transform Your Marriage: Love Lab Experts Share Their Strategies for Strengthening Your Relationship.* Random House.

Inghilleri, L. and Solomon, M. (2010). *Exceptional Service, Exceptional Profit: The Secrets of Building a Five-Star Customer Service Organization.* AMACOM Press.

Acknowledgments

I am thankful to many people for supporting me during the writing of my earlier book, *MarriageBiz*. This book, *Relationship Repair for Couples,* and the concept of Dr. Stephanie's Relationship Repair Shop has been over five years in the making.

I am thankful to my number one, Mr. Brendan Knarr, for encouraging me. I think my marriage to Brendan is a great example of having a Relationship Repair Counter even though we sometimes jump over the counter and start battling it out! As a business person, Brendan was instrumental by incorporating some of his ideas and points of view regarding both personal and business relationships to the Relationship Repair concept.

In addition to my husband, Marsha and Candice Knarr helped me care for baby Gavin during the early drafts of *MarriageBiz* and *Relationship Repair.* My "Relationship Repair Shop" ideas were built, in part, from the support of the Knarr family with Brendan fighting for me all the way. Brendan's business input helped me make great strides as we restructured my business back in 2009 and continued with a plan for growth. Bill and Marsha assisted with helping to set up my Relationship Repair Shop in a separate entrance of our nice home.

This *Relationship Repair* project was in a holding pattern due to some life challenges that Brendan and I faced in the spring of 2014, my parents, Leon and Jean Weiland, stepped in. My dad said, "It seems like you could use a little boost here." He was getting into the business of writing and public speaking himself and gave me some additional support. My mom is my other therapist, and of course their help in our home has assisted me in developing my career and business goals.

My brother and his wife, Carl and Jennifer Weiland, also supported me with graphic design help and a promotional video during the earlier stages of this project. When it comes to Relationship Repair, the Weilands can jump over the Relationship Repair Counter with great ease, but ultimately we end up back in our proper place humbly behind the Relationship Service Counter. I know I am incredibly blessed to be part of a family that has the ability to listen, reconcile, and forgive each other even though it is sometimes turbulent getting to that point.

I would also like to acknowledge four professional colleagues who reviewed my earlier drafts: Dr. Carol Werlinich, licensed clinical marriage and family therapist and professor at the University of Maryland Marriage and Family Therapy program reviewed the book, gave me encouragement, and shared constructive feedback for improvement.

Merlene Blair-Brown, licensed clinical marriage and family therapist of Owings Mills, Maryland, also reviewed my work and encouraged me.

While completing research, I happily discovered that Dr. John Curtis, author of *The Business of Love,* has some similar ideas about using business concepts to create more successful marriages. He graciously agreed to review and support my concepts too.

Finally, Djarta Halliday completed some of the early research, reviewed a first draft of the book, and shared constructive feedback to improve it.

I also must acknowledge my many loyal clients who have learned from my Relationship Repair metaphors. At times, couples commented that the examples helped them better communicate with each other. I have learned many things from my couples who willingly share their hearts and make themselves vulnerable. It is an honor to learn about the ups and downs of marriage from such wonderful people.

Most importantly, although I am respectful of the many diverse beliefs of my clients and acquaintances, I cannot give thanks without acknowledging my own relationship with Christ who called me to serve married couples and families. Only God truly knows my deepest heart and all my unique struggles to write *Relationship Repair for Couples.* So, to God, I am thankful for helping me to hold onto the light of Christ in the midst of some dark moments in my life personally and professionally during the past decade.

About Dr. Stephanie

———◆———

Stephanie Weiland Knarr, PhD, LCMFT, is a licensed clinical marriage and family therapist. She is a Professional Member of the National Speakers Association.

She has been the owner of Stephanie Weiland, LLC, her well-respected marriage and family therapy practice in Metropolitan Washington, D.C., since 2002. Stephanie received her PhD from St. Mary's University of San Antonio, Texas, in Counseling and Human Services, with an emphasis in Marriage and Family Therapy, in 2001. In 1999, Stephanie completed a Master of Science Degree at Colorado State University in Human Development and Family Studies, with an emphasis in Marriage and Family Therapy. Her Bachelor's degree in Psychology is from Creighton University in Omaha, Nebraska. Stephanie has completed training in EMDR, and she has completed Level 1 and Level 2 Trainings with the Gottman Institute. She is working towards her credentials to be a Gottman Certified Marriage Therapist. Dr. Stephanie Weiland Knarr has been quoted as an expert in *Time*, *Forbes*, and *MSN*. Her professional research and study has earned her publication in the Journal of Marital and Family Therapy, Contemporary Family Therapy, and the Journal of Child and Adolescent and Group Therapy. In the past, she has presented at the National Council on Family Relations, the American Association for Marriage and Family Therapy Annual Conference, and for the American Counseling Association Annual Conference.

Raised on a Nebraska farm, she brings the down-to-earth family values and work ethic from America's Midwest to her family therapy business.

Dr. Stephanie lives with her husband, Brendan Knarr, in Maryland. They are co-directing their family organization and raising three children: Rachel, Luke, and Gavin.

Contact Dr. Stephanie Weiland Knarr through her website at www.drstephanieonline.com.